The French Resistance and Its Legacy

The French Resistance and Its Legacy

ROD KEDWARD

BLOOMSBURY ACADEMIC
LONDON • NEW YORK • OXFORD • NEW DELHI • SYDNEY

BLOOMSBURY ACADEMIC
Bloomsbury Publishing Plc
50 Bedford Square, London, WC1B 3DP, UK
1385 Broadway, New York, NY 10018, USA
29 Earlsfort Terrace, Dublin 2, Ireland

BLOOMSBURY, BLOOMSBURY ACADEMIC, and the Diana logo are trademarks
of Bloomsbury Publishing Plc

First published in Great Britain 2022

Cover design by Tjaša Krivec
Resistance Call circa 1944: The telephone operator at Boussoulet, in the Haute Loire,
helps members of the Maquis or French Resistance who use a code between telephone
operators to report the movements of the German forces. (© Keystone/Getty Images).

A catalogue record for this book is available from the British Library.

A catalog record for this book is available from the Library of Congress.

ISBN: HB: 978-1-3502-6043-6
PB: 978-1-3502-6042-9
ePDF: 978-1-3502-6044-3
eBook: 978-1-3502-6045-0

Typeset by Deanta Global Publishing Services, Chennai, India
Printed and bound in Great Britain

To find out more about our authors and books visit www.bloomsbury.com and
sign up for our newsletters.

For Isabella, Niamh, Lucien, and Rufus

Contents

Illustrations

Figures

Maps

Foreword

Increasingly in the first twenty years of the twenty-first century, the concept of "resistance" in history and world affairs has expanded to include movements of protest and actions of ethnic, social, and generational groups which have previously been marginalized or simply disregarded. As the exercise of unregulated power has come under wider scrutiny, so the width and visibility of resistance has become increasingly apparent.

At the same time the tales and tails of history have been given prominence in the passion for commemorations and memory: tales as a synonym for stories, and tails as the afterwords of events through testimony handed down across generations.

This evocation of research into the French Resistance and its legacy evaluates the place of resistance in both history and memory, and one which, at the end, underlines the necessity of resistance studies, and the expanding role of Archives of Resistance Testimony.

Chapter 1 is an introduction both to my pursuit of resistance in France since I began research in the late 1960s, and to the growing significance of oral history.

Chapters 2 to 8 signal ways in which resistance has been approached in the last twenty years through a diversity of situations, new ideas, and new material. I have underlined occasions devoted to discussion and exploration, and events of collective commemoration and debate. The aim is to show the excitement and challenge which the study of resistance has created and the pressing need for a criterion of its place in the canon of historical activity.

In this ever-widening pursuit since the 1960s I have continued to owe everything to resisters themselves, to the inspiring family presence and ideas of Carol, Joshua and Jessica across the decades, and to friends, students, and colleagues in the UK, France, the USA, and elsewhere, to all of whom this little book, with its celebration of memory in history, is warmly and gratefully dedicated.

Rod Kedward, March 2021

Acknowledgments

Photos

In 2019 when I first started to put this book together I relied notably on the experience of others on how and where to obtain photographs of locally known resisters and their activity. I now wish to acknowledge with gratitude the many suggestions made by Martyn Cox which led to Louise Bibbey and the Maquis d'Ornano photos, and the names supplied by Robert Pike which took me to Alan Latter and his website collection of images of a maquis in the Dordogne. Both Louise and Alan have kindly given their permission for their photos to be used here as have Getty Images and Topfoto, for which I am equally grateful.

I also wish to acknowledge Suzanne Hodgart's immense experience of pictorial research which has been such a constant stimulus, and the photographic skills of Stuart Robinson which he provided so generously and creatively.

Text

I will be permanently grateful to Oxford University Press for their publication in 1978 and 1993 of my research which contained oral interviews with individual resisters, and to Champ Vallon and Éditions du Cerf for the translations published in 1989 and 1999. For the first of these two French publications I am very grateful for the input and support of Jean-Pierre Azéma and the Institut d'Histoire du Temps Présent, and for the second I am particularly indebted to the initiative and insights of Alya Aglan. The original versions of most of the interviews have now been digitized and are available to readers and researchers at the University of Sussex Archive of Resistance Testimony, which is directed by Chris Warne and benefits hugely from the generosity of Nick Elverston.

A few of the chapters below contain passages which have appeared before in volumes edited by others, or were lectures given at academic occasions. I particularly wish to acknowledge that material on Georges Guingouin in Chapter 5 first appeared in Heiko Feldner, Claire Gorrara, and Kevin Passmore (eds), *The Lost Decade? The 1950s in European History, Politics, Society and Culture*, Cambridge Scholars Publishing, 2011, while most of Chapter 6 appeared originally as *The Pursuit of Reality: the Némirovsky Effect*, the Stenton Lecture, which was kindly circulated in print by the University of Reading in 2008.

Finally, I wish to acknowledge the constant support, advice and suggestions of Bloomsbury editors Rhodri Moxford and Laura Reeves.

Abbreviations

AS   **Armée Secrète.** The military organization of resistance, ultimately within the MUR, organizing both maquis units and groupes francs.

BCRA(M) **Bureau Central de Renseignements et d'Action (Militaire).** The intelligence and action network of de Gaulle's France Libre (later France Combattante), initially run from London by André Dewavrin (Colonel Passy).

CIMADE **Comité intermouvements auprès des évacués.** Humanitarian body of Protestant origin before the war, which became closely involved with the plight and escape of refugees and children interned in Vichy camps, especially Gurs.

CDL   **Comité Départemental de Libération.** Liberation committee of each département, often nominated secretly as early as the winter of 1943–4.

CNR   **Conseil National de la Résistance.** National Council of the Resistance, the ultimate political achievement of de Gaulle's emissary Jean Moulin, aimed at uniting the resistance within France. The CNR charter for post-Liberation France was launched in March 1944.

FFI   **Forces Françaises de l'Intérieur.** The official, and at first largely theoretical, merging of all armed resistance into one military organization under General Koenig, dating from the end of 1943 but operative mainly in the spring and summer of 1944.

FLN   **Front de Libération Nationale.** Algerian National Liberation Front, formed in 1954.

FN   **Front National.** The wide-based resistance movement initiated by the Communist Party in the summer of 1941, and operating in both zones as a military and political organization, open to all volunteers whether communist or not.

FTP(F)   **Francs-Tireurs et Partisans (Français).** The armed forces of the FN, led nationally by Charles Tillon.

GF   **Groupes Francs.** Action units, formed mostly within Combat as early as 1941, and later acting as urban groups as distinct from the rural maquis.

GMR   **Groupes Mobiles de Réserve.** Vichy paramilitary police.

IHTP   **Institut d'Histoire du Temps Présent.** National Institute of Contemporary History.

MOI   **Main d'Oeuvre Immigrée.** Communist organization dating from before the war to represent immigrant workers.

MUR   **Mouvements Unis de la Résistance.** The unified organization, dating from January 1943, of three movements of resistance in the southern (Vichy) zone: Combat, Libération (sud), and Franc-Tireur.

NAP   **Noyautage des Adminstrations Publiques.** An activity created by Combat to infiltrate and destabilize public administration.

OSE   **Oeuvre de secours aux enfants.** Humanitarian body providing social and medical help for Jewish children in need.

OSS   **Office of Strategic Services.** American secret service, sending agents into Occupied France.

PCF   **Parti Communiste Français.** French Communist Party.

SNCF   **Société Nationale des Chemins de Fer Français.** French national railways.

SOE   **Special Operations Executive.** Secret British organization set up to wage war behind enemy lines. F section was independent of de Gaulle and France Libre; RF section worked closely with France Libre and the BCRA. The two sections kept themselves distinct and both sent agents into France. So too did the British MI6, a synonym for SIS, the Secret (or Special) Intelligence Service.

STO   **Service du Travail Obligatoire.** Compulsory labor service fully promulgated in February 1943 to send young French workers to Germany.

UFF   **Union des Femmes Françaises.** Recalling the movement prominent in the Paris Commune of 1971, it was re-formed in mid-1944, closely linked to the Communist Party.

Maps

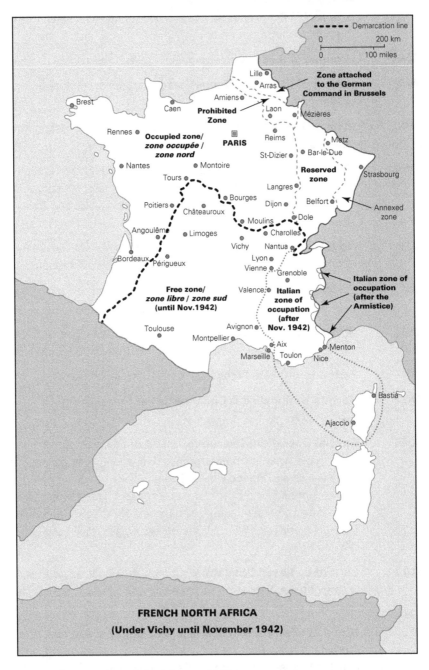

Demarcation line

0   200 km

0   100 miles

Lille

Arras

Zone attached to the German Command in Brussels

Amiens

Brest

Caen

Prohibited Zone

Laon

Mézières

Rennes

Occupied zone/ zone occupée / zone nord

PARIS

Reims

Metz

St-Dizier

Bar-le-Due

Nantes

Montoire

Tours

Reserved zone

Langres

Strasbourg

Poitiers

Bourges

Dijon

Belfort

Châteauroux

Moulins

Dole

Annexed zone

Angoulême

Limoges

Charolles

Bordeaux

Périgueux

Vichy

Nantua

Lyon

Vienne

Grenoble

Free zone/ zone libre / zone sud (until Nov.1942)

Valence

Italian zone of occupation (after Nov. 1942)

Italian zone of occupation (after the Armistice)

Toulouse

Avignon

Montpellier

Aix

Menton

Marseille

Toulon

Nice

Bastia

Ajaccio

FRENCH NORTH AFRICA

(Under Vichy until November 1942)

MAP 1 *The zones imposed on France, 1940.*

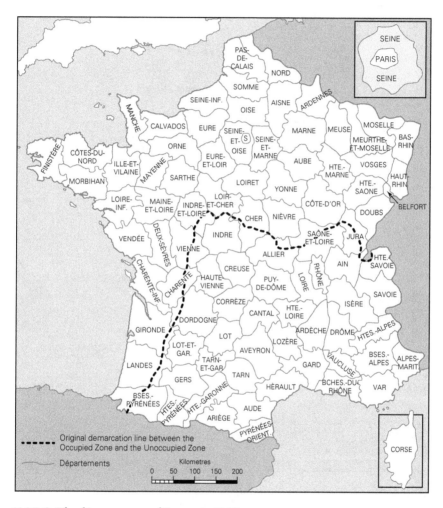

MAP 2 *The départements of France in 1940.*

MAP 3 *The regions of France in 1940.*

1

Introduction

A Pursuit of Resistance

L et me begin, in the words of Julian Barnes, with the sense of an ending.
That ending was the Liberation of France in 1944 which, at its seventieth anniversary in 2014 was widely celebrated and newly documented. In London, the Institut Français (French Institute) hosted a two-day conference of French and British historians organized by Hanna Diamond and Robert Gildea, Ludivine Broch, and Daniel Lee, while there was, and still is, a highly original and revealing collection of French books and images, published in the period from the Liberation of Paris in 1944 to the end of 1946, made by Charles Chadwyck-Healey and donated to Cambridge University Library. A dramatic and evocative selection of these was exhibited at the Library with a catalog entitled *Literature of the Liberation*.

In France, as a major part of the anniversary, President François Hollande spoke in the Mediterranean port of Toulon. He saluted the memory of General de Gaulle's Free French movement which started in London and honored its indigenous recruits from North Africa and beyond, and he remembered the resisters inside France whose active resistance had helped to make it possible for him to echo de Gaulle's declaration that "France had liberated itself."

That had been the message of the general in 1944 at the consummation of the liberation of Paris when he spoke passionately at the Hôtel de Ville on August 25, 1944: "Paris! Paris humiliated! Paris broken! Paris martyrized! But now Paris liberated! Liberated by herself, by her own people with the help of the armies of France, with the support and aid of France as a whole, of fighting France, of the one and only France, of the true France, of eternal France."

He made no mention of the Allied armies or agents. Not a word about them until four days later in a radio broadcast. But no explicit mention either of the four years of internal resistance, an omission which President Hollande did not repeat.

Two years later, on May 8, 2016, Victory in Europe Day (VE day), the *Guardian* newspaper carried quotes and stories from around Europe on how individuals remember the victory over Nazi Germany. Angelique Chrisafis, the French correspondent for the paper, whose interests are notably local and individual, quoted 94-year-old Marie-Catherine Bovis who had been a student in Aix-en-Provence in May 1945:

> At the time, she said, I didn't know the full horror of the death camps . . . but we were aware of the terrible fact of Jewish people being denounced and deported. I had a Jewish uncle who only just escaped deportation. It was only down to a village post lady that he survived. She came across a letter to the authorities from a villager denouncing him as a Jew and she destroyed it.

This was not a military memory of May 8, not a national one, but a local and individual memory of an act of resistance.

The staggering defeat of France and the trauma experienced by the whole nation had, on July 10, 1940, led the National Assembly to place all power in the hands of Marshal Philippe Pétain, the 84-year-old general, known since the First World War as the "Victor of Verdun." He had succeeded Paul Reynaud as prime minister on June 16, 1940, and had called for a cease-fire on the following day. This had led to an Armistice imposed by Germany and signed by the new French government. France was divided by the Armistice into different zones. The fully occupied northern zone had Paris as its center and included the whole of the western coastline. It was separated by a guarded demarcation line from the southern, free zone (*zone sud* or *zone libre*), which was nominally unoccupied. It was in this zone that Marshal Pétain's government abolished the Republic and created an *État* (State) whose rule, in principle, covered the whole of France but was run from the spa town of Vichy, with Pétain as its leader (*Chef*) and Pierre Laval as the first prime minister. The Vichy regime with Pétain still at its head continued after Germany occupied the whole of the south in November 1942, in response to the Allied invasion of North Africa. Germany's ally, Mussolini's Italy, had been allotted a small eastern strip of the *zone sud* to occupy, but this was enlarged in November 1942 to include Corsica and most of the mainland provinces east of the Rhône. This area returned to German occupation when Italy changed sides in the autumn of 1943. By then Corsica had been liberated, but the occupation of the whole of mainland France intensified. So too did the meaning of collaboration. At the start it was portrayed as a necessary policy of administrative cooperation between Vichy and the occupiers, but in 1943–4 its meaning hardened in a police hunt by Vichy for those refusing the compulsory draft of French labor to Germany (*STO*) and by a military repression of the Resistance. The armed Vichy Milice under Joseph Darnand allied itself closely to the German forces in attacks on the maquis groups in the hills, forests, and mountains, backed by the highly effective radio propaganda of Philippe Henriot who labeled the Resistance as a terrorist avant-garde of a planned Bolshevik, Jewish, and Russian takeover.

The very first series of decrees of the Vichy state made Jews second-class citizens or worse, and in many areas they were pursued relentlessly. The local French police were used across the whole of France in roundups and arrests, and in some areas combined with the Germans in the first mass deportations. Where exactly the Jews, mainly immigrant ones, were being taken, in appalling, bestial conditions, was unknown, but the Vichy government, and Laval in particular, made no attempt to find out. A total of 76,000 Jews were deported, of whom only 2,600 survived.

The act of the post lady near Aix-en-Provence was subversive. It defied Vichy legality, but it had its own moral legitimacy. Defiance was frequently a humanitarian act of protest, and one of the very first personal accounts I read in 1968 was by Françoise Meifredy, whose clandestine notebooks were published in 1966. On June 21, 1940, as the German troops rapidly moved south toward Lyon, she discovered a pile of Senegalese soldiers killed by the Germans for refusing to surrender their arms and massacred in a field just outside Lyon. "We made a trench and filled it with the bodies," she wrote, and in the succeeding days she helped several wounded black soldiers to places of safety, despite German orders that anyone helping or burying black soldiers would be severely punished.[1]

Acts by individuals and small groups, and collective action by distinctive movements and networks (*mouvements, réseaux*), were the essence of internal resistance in France until 1943–4 when dispersed armed struggle, identified mainly with the rural *maquis* and urban *groupes francs* (irregular forces), escalated to the creation of the unified *Forces françaises de l'Intérieur* (*FFI*).

One Enemy Only–The Invader was the translated title of Paul Simon's book in 1942, stressing the unity of France in its fight against the Nazi occupation. De Gaulle in London wrote a short preface, ending with words thanking the author for revealing "the true France, which is today suffering but militant, and tomorrow will be triumphant."[2] But in reality there was not one enemy but two: the Occupiers (both German and Italian) and the French collaborators, a reality which became more and more venomous and divisive between 1942 and 1944.

In a little book issued in advance of D-Day by the British Foreign Office titled *Instructions for British Servicemen in France 1944* and prepared in secret by The Political Warfare Executive, a section called "France since 1940" contained the following words:

active resistance, starting immediately after the collapse, from small isolated groups, has organized itself in the teeth of the Gestapo, the German army and Vichy, into a highly efficient network covering the whole of France. It recognized a central authority, and its members regarded themselves as soldiers under military orders. Frenchmen who have risked everything in these resistance groups feel that they have done all that lay in their power to redeem the disgrace of their country's collapse in 1940 by fighting on as our active allies. So, before reminding a Frenchman that France let us down in 1940, remind yourself that you are speaking to one of the thousands of soldiers, without uniform, who have been fighting the same fight as you against the same enemy, but with fewer advantages.

In many ways this was a good little introduction to what had been happening in France, although even in its own time it could have said French men *and women* "who have risked everything," and it could have underlined that these were overwhelmingly civilian volunteers. But, given that its intended readership was military, it successfully alerted British soldiers to the phenomenon of "fighters without uniforms."

Military history since then has not always helped to build on these instructions of 1944 and advance a fuller understanding of internal French Resistance. It needs to acknowledge that resistance was a type of struggle that was linked to protest and revolution, as well as war, and had its own distinctive characteristics. It was clandestine or underground, whichever word is preferred, and it was subversive and transgressive in the eyes of the occupying forces and the repressive powers of the Vichy authority. Resistance, which was always by a minority of French people, had all these characteristics in addition to its military and intelligence capacity; it often failed in its own high ideals and was often helpless against the overwhelming odds.

Just how important it is to contrast resistance with the norms of soldiering has been well captured by Sébastien Albertelli, the historian of the Gaullist network in London, the BCRA (*Bureau Central de Renseignements et d'Action*), who emphasizes that special agents sent into France had to adopt the transgressive behavior of the internal, voluntary resisters. They had to recognize the specific risks of clandestine combat, such as torture and suicide, as well as the greater freedom of maneuver which was not experienced by combatants in regular units.[3]

Resisters I have interviewed mostly minimized their own courage or heroism, but all have made sure that I know of co-resisters, friends and colleagues, comrade partisans and maquisards, who had been tortured, killed, or deported.

Volunteer resisters were no more than a few thousand in 1940–1, in dispersed, like-minded clusters, but by 1944 the internal Resistance was known as *L'armée des ombres* (the shadow army) and featured many foreigners from Poland, Spain, Eastern Europe, and Germany itself, and numbered between 400,000 and 500,000, actively engaged with or without arms, plus equal numbers or more who were collusive in their support or occasional acts.

It is estimated that 35,000 resisters lost their lives. Unknown numbers, but running into thousands, were tortured, and we do not have an accurate number of suicides. As for the military contribution of the Resistance, it was estimated by US generals as worth 10 divisions, equal to some 140,000 uniformed troops.

I began my research in the late 1960s in the *zone sud* (Vichy zone) of France. I looked at grassroots resisters, their individual personalities, background, ideas, and motivation. Why did they resist? And why these specific places where they had resisted? Towns first of all, then rural areas later.

Imagine a warm September day in the Périgord region in 1972, outside a little town between Bergerac and Bordeaux. I was interviewing a local notable and ex-royalist, Louis de la Bardonnie, a French equivalent of an eccentric squire out of the Henry Fielding novel, *Tom Jones*. He made me steal a notice from the outside wall of the local police station before he would agree to talk, and then made me put it back, and finally, we sat down for a day's interview. He was one of the very few who claimed to have heard de Gaulle's first BBC broadcast (*Appel*) of June 18, 1940. He immediately started spying on German ships in and out of Bordeaux. De la Bardonnie became a bastion of the important resistance network run by Colonel Rémy (Gilbert Renault) called Confrérie Notre Dame (CND), covering the whole of the Atlantic coast. He had reinvented himself as a secret intelligence agent. The Germans were in France: he was already behind enemy lines. Where better? Who better, with the cover of his right-wing ideas and prominent social standing?

The next day I met a retired priest, the curé Alvitre, in the Corrèze, who was proud of being a "red priest," whose subversive resistance ideas and actions were denounced by his superiors, and who worked closely in Brive with a younger priest, the abbé Laire, who was arrested and shot for keeping a radio transmitter in his belfry. "I sheltered many people," Alvitre said, "Jews, Resisters, anyone who was being hunted."

The year before, I had met Madeleine Baudoin in Marseille. As an eighteen-year-old student she had been contemptuous of public passivity in 1940 and was excoriating about the public adulation for Pétain. She joined an armed urban group and rejected any compromise. Hers was a war against fascism, she said, it was "an international fight."

She introduced me to Joseph Pastor, who had been imprisoned by the French government as "a notorious Communist" but who defied the party's official support for the Nazi–Soviet pact of Non-Aggression signed in August 1939, and started to rebuild the party secretly in Marseille, with acts of sabotage of material going to Germany.

In 1969 I had interviewed André Plaisantin, a building engineer in 1940 and a humanitarian Christian Democrat, in Lyon. One of the first to form a group of the movement Combat, he initiated the scheme of keeping resisters in their civil service jobs to provide information and means of sabotage at the core of the Vichy administration. Known as the NAP (*Noyautage des administrations publiques*, Infiltration of Public Services), it was hugely creative and successful. The "post lady" near Aix-en-Provence may well have been in the NAP. Alban Vistel was another engineer and was my first contact in Lyon. He used the cover of training a football team to create his own cluster of resisters. He became a significant leader in the southeast, and wrote of the "Spiritual Heritage of the Resistance."

Albert Solié and Frédéric Montagné were communist trade union workers in the Fouga metalworks in the southern town of Béziers. They restarted their banned union and published its newsletter clandestinely. They met at the home of a barrister, Pierre Malafosse, whom I was also able to interview on a hot summer's day in 1970 at an intriguing address on the Mediterranean coast at the Cap d'Agde. It turned out to be a nudist camp. He started by saying he couldn't care a damn about the past; my tape recorder broke down; my companion, Albert Solié, was sweating profusely with the heat and embarrassment, and kept trying to loosen his tie which he had worn out of respect for his bourgeois advocate, but all finally went well. Pierre Malafosse began to give us his testimony, the tape was made, and ended with his words: "I had plenty of money, an important facility in my resistance activity. I became a resister, I suppose, because I was against Hitler, but chance had a lot to do with it."

If often did—an important fact in early resistance, and a frequent admission in interviews. But conviction was more important.

Imaginative thinking, subversive action, gathering intelligence, mobilizing others, secretly writing, printing, and distributing formed the creative bedrock of the "armée des ombres." Liberation was the keyword and republican "Liberté" its legendary inspiration; sabotage was its signature; dissimulation, covering tracks, was its artistry; interlocking urban streets and eventually the hills and woods were its habitat; providing sanctuary and means of escape was its ethical core. Approximately 4,000 surviving Allied aircrew, downed in combat, were given refuge and were taken across the country and over frontiers to safety. Men and women teachers in small schools hid material in their desks, and individual Jewish children in the basement.

In the 1980s and early 1990s I moved from the first two years of southern resistance to search for the local histories of the maquis groups in the woods and hills, tracking down the culture of the outlaw and the specific significance of place and time, as well as continuing to discover individual motivation. The places known for collective refuge and combat are among the acknowledged citadels of resistance (*hauts-lieux de la Résistance*). They still need meticulous research, and their stories still need telling.

Above all, clichés and generalizations have to be avoided, but much is to be gained from studying how certain anniversary commemorations reveal shifting emphases and directions in pursuit of new understanding. The years leading up to the fiftieth anniversary of the Liberation in 1994 were particularly marked by the call to remember resistance for its failures as well as its successes, for actions which should be deplored as well as those that need rescuing from neglect. These included the instances when German prisoners of war were shot or badly treated by resistance groups, the summary executions of collaborators, and the male violence exhibited in the parading of women accused of sexual relations with the enemy and the atavistic shaving of their heads. Ex-resisters I interviewed in these years included Francis Cammaerts, at his rural home in the département of the Drôme in southeast France. This celebrated special agent, code-named Roger, of the British SOE (Secret Operations Executive) was as careful with his judgments and memories as he had been in organizing his resistance groups, and he acknowledged the need to recognize the negative aspects of the resistance story. Yet at the same time he offered no apology for saying, "There was something extraordinarily civilized about the Liberation. Far too little has been written about it." This was not a cliché or a generalization. He specified "something." But how much was that "something" and how central was it to the identity not only of the Liberation but also of the four years of resistance which preceded it?

Francis Cammaerts expressed his belief with the passion of someone who wants to enlighten researchers and not just inform them, but it was not an ex-cathedra statement made out of context. We had discussed numerous angles of resistance motivation, action, and ideas throughout the day, and had come to the difficult questions of courage, dedication, anger, and revenge in the armed struggle which led to the various local liberations, in the plural, at different moments in the summer of 1944 after the Allied invasion on D-Day. Cammaerts had outlined the ambushes and sabotage from June 6 to August 15 which had cleared the Alpine roads. "It was an amazing achievement by the Resistance," he said, and he added, "It has to be repeated over and over again: by the time the Allies invaded the Alpine regions there wasn't any fighting. It had all been done. In terms of lives saved, both Allied and German, it was an enormous achievement." He then retold the concern expressed by a young maquisard who asked him how much food and exercise he should give to his 300 German prisoners according to international conventions. It was not only the success of the resistance activity in his region in saving lives, but also this individual, humanitarian concern that he did not want to be forgotten. That was when he used the phrase "something extraordinarily civilized."[4]

It echoed other stories that I had already met in interviews and archival research. For example, in the small southern town of Saint-Pons in the Hérault, a local doctor, Joseph Bec, treated the injured maquisards and Germans equally, thereby saving the town from destruction by the retreating German commander who had originally threatened to kill all the inhabitants. A similar scenario was enacted in the town of Ussel in the Haute-Corrèze where the German wounded spoke up for the care shown to them by the surgeon Jean Boisselet and his local staff.

Tangentially, the departmental archives reveal a larger minority than is sometimes recognized of resisters on the local Liberation Committees who expressed their hostility to the shaving (*tontes*) of women's heads and the treatment of suspected collaborators. Dr. Benedettini in the Gard declared that the *tontes* had "done us so much harm," and Dr. Arène went further and claimed that the degrading treatment had "lost us the benefit of all we have done over four years." Such individual protests give substance to the poem and engravings in 1945–6 by Anna Prinner who was outraged at the savagery of the shavings. I have only recently encountered her work: it now features in Chadwyck-Healey's collected "Literature of the Liberation" at Cambridge.

How isolated were these moral protests at the moment of Liberation? There were incidents of negotiation with the Germans for their withdrawal, as in Limoges, or the determined avoidance of inter-resistance violence and bloodshed at the Liberation, as argued in a high moral tone by the Sub-Prefect of Villefranche-de-Rouergue and Decazeville in the Aveyron. Do they belong in the same category as the moral essentialism of Camus's *Lettres à un ami allemand* ("Letters to a German Friend") started in 1943, or the wider meaning of Eluard's words in April 1944 referring to *notre victoire sur la mort* ("Our Victory Over Death")?

And how do they relate to the words of another celebrated SOE agent, Harry Rée, like his friend Cammaerts a conscientious objector at the start of the war, who claimed that the resistance sabotage of the Peugeot factory in Montbéliard, was "a good job for a conchie," sparing the town from Allied bombing. Still more, what civilized gestures were encompassed in the expectations of radical social change as fleshed out by the CNR, created by Jean Moulin, in its Common Program adopted unanimously in March 1944?

Such questions were foremost in the links made by the ex-resister Stéphane Hessel in his forthright pamphlet *Indignez-vous!* ("Time for Outrage!"), which made a fundamental connection between the CNR Program and the United Nations Declaration of Human Rights, of which he was a coeditor, in 1948.[5] At the age of ninety-two he made a profound impact on a week of events in London in 2010 which celebrated the seventieth anniversary of de Gaulle's first BBC broadcast to France on June 18, 1940. He repeatedly affirmed the unity of moral purpose in the Resistance, whatever its real or apparent internal disagreements and complexity. His convictions, which he relayed tirelessly over decades to schools and meetings all over France, had a public impact which cannot be overestimated.

Stéphane Hessel died at the end of February 2013, aged ninety-five, just a few months before France decided that an annual National Day (*Journée nationale*) to commemorate the Resistance should be proclaimed for May 27, beginning in 2014. It would not be a national holiday but it was felt to be the best date to celebrate the Resistance as a unity. The first clandestine meeting of the CNR had been held on May 27, 1943, in the rue du Four in Paris.

In open pursuit of the many sides to the resistance story, the "army of the shadows" has to be recognized as such. The shadows were its strength. At the same time the story needs to be brought out of the shadows, and out of the footnotes of military history, if its distinctiveness is to be understood. Resistance, in France and elsewhere, needs its own historical category. The following chapters lead to a conclusion that confronts this necessity. Here and there they are followed by short extracts from a few recorded interviews, which allow a range of voices to be heard.

*   *   *

Arriving in Lyon in the summer of 1969, I was put in touch with Alban Vistel who had been the regional head of the MUR. He greeted me on August 10 with a copy of his 1955 meditation on resistance, titled Héritage spirituel de la Résistance. *He traced his own resistance back to a firm humanitarian commitment well before the war.*

M. Alban VISTEL

I was thirty-nine in 1940 and was living just outside Lyon. I had never been a member of a political party, yet had formed strong political convictions. For five years in the early 1930s I had lived in South America where I was made acutely aware of social problems and human misery. It was where I began my career as a conspirator. I felt I was being prepared for something but didn't know what. When the Civil War in Spain started I was emotionally involved on the Republican side due to the Spanish-American origins of my wife, as well as my anti-Nazi ideas. I would have gone to fight as a volunteer but my wife was pregnant.

I was an engineer in a small factory. I never identified with the employers, but my position made me a mediator between the employers and the unions. I was the only member of the General Trade Union movement, the CGT, and had marched in favor of the Popular Front in the 1930s singing the *Internationale*.

In educational terms I had had a legal and scientific university training, but my vocation was for the humanities. I had moved away from religion, and my passion was for "revolution." I wanted to change the world. Everything else was secondary, and I valued literature only if it shed light on man's condition.

I had seen the realities of colonization and I was convinced that capitalism was incapable of resolving the current economic problems.

When war arrived I declared it to be a just war against an inhuman enemy. I was mobilized in the reserve army and given command of a fortress in the Alps near Grenoble. I saw no action. The defeat was a thunderbolt. It was easy for the vast majority of the French to accept Pétain as a savior. I became determined to do something constructive. I collected young workers from my factory and in November 1940 held my first secret meeting in a disused sports stadium with about fifteen young people. I had read some of Churchill's and de Gaulle's speeches, and I was certain that the scandalous Nazi–Soviet pact would not last.

Resistance was individual and spontaneous at this time and the main problem for me was to keep hold of my circle of young workers by holding regular meetings, typing out tracts, and writing slogans on walls. I had meager means at my disposal but I pretended to have contact with London. It was essential to say this; otherwise, I would have lost my support.

In November 1941 I decided to cycle from my home to see Emmanuel Mounier who was trying to keep his philosophical publication, *Esprit*, alive in the face of censorship. He was very friendly and suggested I should join the movement Libération through André Philip who was my old professor at the Law Faculty. From that point I received packets of clandestine newspapers and I began to reconstruct my following into groups of six. Within Libération there were a good number of Jews and intellectuals, while among the grassroots there were trade-unionists and workers who had left the Communist Party at the time of the Nazi–Soviet pact. One of the most important sources of support were left-wing Catholics from before the war. Resistance as I knew it was essentially an anti-Fascist activity by left-wing people, even anarchists in the best sense of the word. Resistance was a sense of Utopia, even if serious-minded people at the time saw such resistance as mad and ridiculous.[6]

Three years later, on September 20, 1972, I met Louis de la Bardonnie, of similar age to Alban Vistel, at his home in Saint-Antoine-de-Breuilh, in the Dordogne. He was well known locally for his talks and speeches on the Resistance, and his combination of authority and humor. He was determined that younger people should learn about the Resistance. He had written notes on his war years, but no publication was envisaged at that moment. He talked for almost two hours, with two large dogs outside the room needing attention from time to time. He wanted me to find out why the film Sink the Bismarck *(1960) had not mentioned his resistance network which, he maintained, had first located the ship's whereabouts off the French coast.*

M. Louis DE LA BARDONNIE

I was thirty-eight in 1940 and the father of eight children. I was a property owner and farmer in the Dordogne, where my family had been for 600 years. I was a man of the Right, a man of order. For me "patrie" and "famille" were the cardinal values.

I stopped subscribing to *L'Action française* when I read the statement of Charles Maurras that Pétain should be followed even if he was wrong. This was totally unacceptable. I entered Resistance from the moment I heard de Gaulle's first broadcast. I did not hear the start, but when I realized what de Gaulle was saying I called out, "We've won the war." I had never heard of de Gaulle until that moment, but immediately contacted seven good friends, all local landowners, and we met on the day the Armistice was declared. We had to do something, but what? We started with trivial actions like turning round signposts on the other side of the demarcation line which was only 8 kilometers away.

We then began to collect details about the Germans in the occupied zone, and through a friend who was a chief pilot in Bordeaux harbor we gained information on all the German ships going in and out of Bordeaux. On July 14, 1940, we took the first batch of information to Switzerland and delivered it to the British Embassy. I myself went with the second batch on August 8, and we made further journeys in September and October. There was no reply, and yet despite the lack of results, our group grew from seven to thirty-two. Finally, we decided to send a 71-year-old priest, abbé Dartein, through Spain to England. With him we sent a number of photographs of German and Italian ships and submarines in Bordeaux. Our earlier information had reached the English and French in London, but they had believed it was too good to be true. The Gaullist movement, France Libre, sent us an envoy in the person of Rémy, and our network became known as CND.

In 1940, resistance was the action of a very small minority, but it became a mass movement overnight after the invasion of Russia in June 1941 when communists suddenly found themselves automatically in the Resistance. There had been some magnificent exceptions before then, but very few, and personally I had not known any. There were a few Socialists at the beginning, but no Radicals. The definition of a Radical is "Red outside, white inside, and always on the side where the bread is buttered." There were several Jesuits in the early Resistance. In November 1940, I met an elderly Jesuit in Bordeaux who confided to me that Hitler would lose the war. Jesuits are always well informed.

During 1940–2 the aim of our network was to do as much harm as possible to Germany, and to Vichy, which was the same thing. In 1941 I was arrested by Vichy after being denounced by a Frenchman in another network. I was imprisoned for four months, but they could find nothing substantive against me. Subsequently, this denunciation and arrest became the rule: the vast majority of those arrested in our network were denounced by fellow Frenchmen and arrested by Vichy. The so-called double game (*double-jeu*) of Vichy was a lie.[7]

M. Henri CORDESSE

Two years before, in September 1970, I interviewed schoolteacher Henri Cordesse, who had become Prefect of the Lozère in the Languedoc at the Liberation. He was preparing to write his account of local resistance, which came out a few years later. He was very reflective about cause and effect and did not attempt to avoid the complexities of choice and behavior. He thought that his early resistance was partly due to being a married man with a family, saying that he felt more responsible for the future of France and a greater need to keep it free from Nazism. I returned to him ten years later, in April 1982, when I was researching the maquis in the southern zone. His second testimony was all-inclusive. Not only did he cover the motivation and activity of the local groups of maquis but he also stressed the support of peasant farmers, postal workers, railway workers, and especially the farmers' wives without whom the resistance "could not have managed; being a mère de famille carried far more responsibility than being a père de famille: their risks and sacrifices were greater."

Earlier in the interview he had addressed the accusation leveled at the maquis, both at the time and since, that they had terrorized the locality:

It was vital for the maquis to establish an aura of force and power. Many people who never took part in an attack or a raid nevertheless welcomed the news that the maquis was doing something active. The maquisards had to create a climate of mystery and effectiveness. They were on the run and had made a political commitment. They had to make an impact. The use of any explosives was crucial for this. Some just enjoyed the sensation of having a pistol in their hands. We couldn't always pick these types out in advance. Our selection process wasn't sophisticated enough. But they were a minority. For most maquisards, however, it was still necessary to feel part of a fighting tradition, to live up to the *images d'Épinal* (popular, legendary images) of hard, tough warriors. And there was the mentality of "war to the bitter end." They were given no quarter by the Germans or the Vichy Milice, so they would show no mercy to the collaborators. It was a terrible mentality. We saw maquisards whose sole aim was to avenge their comrades. This was difficult to keep under control, and it explains the blemishes in our history. There was a level of enthusiasm which is impossible to represent in words. At the Liberation there was a spontaneous demand for justice. How does one account for the same scenes enacted everywhere without any knowledge of what others were doing? Perhaps there is an element of truth in the notion that a victorious army always acts in the same way. The sexual retribution, in the shaving of heads, was occasionally directed against pretty girls who had merely enjoyed going out to the cinema a lot. We touched rock bottom there. It demonstrated how merciless we could be. But such acts were the exception, not the norm.

He concluded:
In the end some of the heroic legends of the maquis are an overselective choice of the facts. They suppress the fear that the maquisards experienced, and they underplay just how hard and difficult it all was."[8]

2

The Discourse of Heroism

Of all the Manichean splits in the twentieth century, that between resisters and collaborators in Occupied France must be one of the most entrenched. All the recent focus on Holocaust studies, the outrage at Holocaust Denial, and the trials of Paul Touvier and Maurice Papon in the 1990s for crimes against humanity confirmed Nazism as a political synonym of evil. Those who actively resisted its power and its blandishments between 1940 and 1944 are therefore still widely defined as its opposite. The discourse of goodness and heroism has marked all stages of the history of resistance. There is no easy periodization of this discourse: it is sometimes prevalent, it is sometimes muted. It captures national headlines and local ceremonials. It has its fierce defenders and fewer but voluble detractors. More consistently present is the discourse of the resistance martyr. The martyrs, often tortured and mutilated, have been monumentalized as the heroic dead, and their heroism is rarely exposed to serious public doubt. An academic biography of one of them, *Pierre Brossolette Un héros de la résistance* by Guillaume Piketty, was admiringly reviewed in the journal *Vingtième Siècle* by one of the most penetrating and thoughtful resistance historians, Jean-Marie Guillon. He started his review with the words, "Pierre Brossolette was not one of the cohort of forgotten heroes . . . this man was not anonymous." The implication is clear: the cohort of unsung resistance heroes and heroines is still to be remembered, perhaps even still to be found. The discourse remains alive and well.

My own journey back into the history of resistance started in 1968, a year which might have seen the death of the heroic discourse of resistance, at least in university circles.

The year 1968 in France was not only the year of revolts by students and workers, known as *les événements* (the events), but it was also the fiftieth anniversary of the end of the First World War. The two were interwoven in the graffiti which began to appear on the walls in the spring of 1968, most obviously the slogan, "*la guerre de moutons*" ("the war of sheep") which pilloried the war of 1914–18 as one where volunteers and recruits were forced to fight in a struggle directed and controlled by the military and political authority and were no more than "sheep to the slaughter." By contrast the actions of those who created the May events of 1968 and those who staged the general strike were held to possess an existentialist and voluntarist quality. The slogan made this point implicitly, and thereby established a libertarian hierarchy of political causes within France: some were unacceptable because they were imposed from above, others were acceptable because they were willed from the base upwards.

Where in this hierarchy did the Resistance of 1940–4 stand? After the war it had been exploited for political ends by both the Gaullist politicians and the Communist Party, and the students of 1968, the *soixantehuitards*, were explicitly critical of both the Gaullist and the Communist heritage. To many of the students and supporters of 1968, the heroic discourse of resistance designated career-successful politicians who were seen to have grounded their moral and political authority in an uncritical self-history of patriotic heroism and nationalist endeavor. It was claimed that this had failed the postwar world, and many ex-resisters, epitomized by Georges Bidault, who had succeeded Jean Moulin in 1943 at the head of the CNR, were accused of endorsing the imperialism and brutality of the Indo-China and Algerian wars, seen to have been fought in the anachronistic and unacceptable belief that France still had a civilizing, imperial mission.

Ambivalence in 1968 was widespread, however, and I was told the story of an astonishing public confession by a graffiti artist who at night had decorated the local war memorial of a village in the Languedoc with a tidily written *guerre de moutons* only to find in the light of morning that he had covered not the side given to the First World War, but the memorial to *Nos martyrs de la Résistance*. He came into the square as people assembled in the café for the evening apéritif and publicly announced that he had misdirected his graffiti: he had no wish to denigrate the heroes of the Resistance, but only the unacceptable war of 1914–18, and he set to work at once to remove the red spray paint, amid considerable astonishment and no shortage of heckling and debate. He was not allowed to respray the other side, nor did he return at some later date to do so. The story, which I have not been able to authenticate, was typical of the kind of improvised street event in which the serious aspirations of 1968 were expressed. It was typical also, I believe, of the contrast between the two wars which was made during the events, alongside the skepticism about famous resisters as career politicians. In the eyes of their critics what many ex-resisters had failed to do was to acknowledge that the liberation movements in Indo-China and Algeria were in essence a continuation of their own struggle against unacceptable authority. But what was not in doubt was the voluntarism of resisters, both those who later became famous and those who had remained unknown and anonymous. What 1968 did, therefore, was not to end the discourse of resistance heroism, which seemed likely at one point, but to push a number of historians into researching the lives and action of unknown and little-known resisters, both male and female. The significance of this new research was manifest in the series of six international conferences on resistance staged in France in the 1990s, when it became apparent just how many resistance historians, in France, in the United Kingdom, in Belgium and the Netherlands, in Italy and in the United States, were all influenced personally by this 1968 perspective.

In fact, for whatever vintage of historian it would have been extraordinary if the original internal resistance in the first two years of Occupation had not been understood as voluntary. Almost all the existing resistance histories and memoirs of the period treated it as such. And it was not only voluntary. To this was also added the aura of the exceptional and the prophetic. Streets all over France had been named after individual resistance figures. Each political party celebrated its own heroes and heroines, and in December 1964 the ashes of Jean Moulin had been transferred to the Panthéon, an apotheosis of the Gaullist tradition which incarnated the individual and voluntary act of Charles de Gaulle on June 18, 1940, and now the role of his most influential envoy into France.

Before 1964 Jean Moulin had stood for no more and no less than any other leader in the history and collective memory of the Resistance. But with the Panthéon ceremony he became the emblematic resistance hero and martyr, his hat and scarf iconic. His clandestine achievements denoted not *la guerre de moutons* but *la guerre des ombres* (war of the shadows) and his death under torture was held to be symbolic of the martyrdom of France.

It was a Gaullist and nationalist gesture above all, but it made resistance available to be established as a paradigm of individual commitment, and it was this that was recast and reinvented in the existentialism and democratization of 1968, which rejected the two dominant mythic interpretations, that of the Gaullist *nation résistante* (resistant nation) and that of the Communist *parti des fusillés* (party of the executed). Both were myths in the functional, mobilizing sense of creating political identities and serving postwar needs. Neither was accurate in the factual sense: the French nation had not resisted in its entirety—the Communist Party had lost many of its members to the firing squads, but not as many as were being claimed. The myths had allowed individuals to place their resistance motivations and achievements in a collective context: they allowed the collectivities of nation and party to honor their activists as representative. Essentially these myths were rejected in 1968 as discourses of power and authority. The first thing I wrote on resistance was called "Beyond the polemics," mainly due to the realization through oral research that resisters in the southern part of France where I was working had a widespread consciousness of resistance in the first two years as a small minority phenomenon, as multifaceted, flawed, polyvalent, and individualistic. This consciousness was permanently at odds, even in open conflict, with the dominant myths. I was not at all surprised at the wide acceptance in France given to the critical 1969 film by Marcel Ophuls, *Le Chagrin et la Pitié* (The Sorrow and the Pity), and to the groundbreaking study by Robert Paxton, *Vichy France, Old Guard and New Order* (1972) despite scattered refusals to accept the way in which they had, in Henry Rousso's memorable words in 1987, "broken the mirror."[1]

As the individuality of early resistance resurfaced in more detail in the 1970s and 1980s, it took on a much more embattled and quixotic nature. The motivations of "patriotism" ascribed to noncommunists and those of "party loyalty" claimed by communists were both insufficient as explanations of early resistance in 1940–1: patriotism in 1940 had largely been monopolized by the cult of Marshal Pétain, while the notion of the "vanguard party" collapsed when it was admitted that the Central Committee and most of the Communist Party did not embark on resistance to the Germans until the second half of 1941, an admission which maverick communists made soon after the war, but which emerged in official communist historiography only in the mid-1990s. So the first individuals to begin acts of resistance had to be more than just patriotic or just members of the party. Their personalities became the subject of close attention. Was resistance even a sign of a personality disorder?

Emmanuel d'Astier, one of the founders of the resistance movement Libération-sud, had led the way in his interview with Marcel Ophuls in 1969 for the film *Le Chagrin et la Pitié* when he claimed that you had to be a bit of a delinquent to be a resister in the early days. Jean Cassou coined the perceptive, and philosophical, interpretation of resistance as an absurd refusal *un refus absurde* and Lucie Aubrac more and more in her lectures to schools emphasized the guile and ruse which she had employed in a series of masquerades which had outwitted the Gestapo. Lucie Aubrac was on the political Left, but as evidence of similar playacting on the political Right, there had been the tall, debonair Jacques Renouvin, an erstwhile reader and follower of the monarchist and reactionary *Action Française*, who had indulged in a series of histrionic acts when setting up his Groupes Francs (Activist Units) in 1941 in the southern zone. At one point he went to Brive to blow up the house of a collaborator and then, after planting his homemade bomb, he dressed up in an ill-fitting priest's *soutane* to lose himself in a religious parade, creating a caricature of a lanky, laughing cleric parading the streets of Brive with his legs and socks absurdly exposed.

Interviewing at the grass roots, I was confronted with endless such stories, most of which were endorsed by other accounts. A code and discourse of resistance as illegal, inventive, imaginative, individualistic, and outrageously defiant circulated alongside the more conventional image of the early resister as the tough and prudent clandestine activist or the armed maquisard in the woods. Many of the descriptions by M. R. D. Foot of agents who were dropped into France by the British organization, the SOE, fell into the category of the idiosyncratic and quixotic. "SOE's work," he wrote at the start of *SOE in France*, his classic study of 1966, "was true to the tradition of English eccentricity; the sort of thing that Captain Hornblower or Mycroft Holmes in fiction, or Admiral Cochrane or Chinese Gordon in fact, would have gone in for had they been faced with a similar challenge; the sort of thing that looks odd at the time, and eminently sensible later." His account has scores of short biographical sketches or comments which add color and detail to this image of SOE's functional eccentricity. There is a coherent discourse of resistance in *SOE in France*. It is the discourse of personality. Generalizing about the SOE agents, Michael Foot continues,

> Their diversity was marked: it ranged from pimps to princesses . . . SOE employed neither supermen or simpletons. Many agents were remarkably good; a few were remarkably bad. Some were foolhardy, some were fusspots; some, not unexpectedly, were odd, like the English captain with several daring operations to his credit, who was brave as a lion in action and drunk as a lord in between; or the Gascon major, also fearless, of whom a staff officer wrote plaintively, "I wish he would not use so much scent."

Michael Foot's writing is open to parody: it appears to indulge in the archetype of the talented amateur, but it nevertheless expresses an intimate and fundamental understanding of SOE which no one has seriously disputed: these were men and women of highly distinctive personalities. It may seem amazing that this treatment of SOE has not been the object of revisionism, but everyone who thinks about it finds it hard to imagine any other way in which to encapsulate the essence of SOE, except in purely structural or functional terms, and Foot was remarkably perceptive too about both structures and functions.[2]

SOE agents, however, were specially recruited: they were chosen to be members of the Special Forces. They were irregulars recruited to do an irregular job. Their role was to a large extent prescribed and they were intensively trained. A certain kind of personality was high on the list of requirements. Foot's discourse of personality is not out of place.

Resisters within France were different: they were not in the first instance recruited. They created their own role: they had to create the very phenomenon of resistance out of their refusal and opposition. This difference had to lead to different questions about motivation, origin, and strategy. It is true that their personalities were in many cases no less eccentric than those of SOE agents, and many memoirs and studies of individual resisters privilege personality over context, substantiating the claim made by Emmanuel d'Astier. After 1968 and *Le Chagrin et la Pitié*, refusal became a key word in the discourse of heroism, and absurdity, used in the philosophical sense, a key but contested concept. Together they made up the idea of *un refus absurde* (an absurd refusal). There was nothing Dostoyevan, still less Nietzschean, about the discourse, nor did it have the anti-hero dimensions of Meursault in the novel *L'Étranger* by Albert Camus in 1942. For reasons Camus gave later in *Lettres à un ami allemand* (Letters to a German Friend), there was no absurdity of moral values in the consciousness of the resister; it was rather the element of contingency in individual revolt that gave refusal its air of absurdity. "*Il fallait faire quelque chose*" ("I had to do something") was and still is the most persistent statement proffered to those researching the first acts of resistance.

I was struck, and still am, at the examples of life imitating art, or in this case, philosophy. André Roure, in 1940 a philosophy student of existentialism, felt he had to do something, so he tried to swim the Channel to join General de Gaulle. Swept back by the first big wave, he was picked up on the beach and sent back to his studies by an indulgent German officer who told him not to be stupid. He became involved in resistance acts, distributing clandestine material, but that wasn't commitment enough. In 1942 he set off to join the French forces in North Africa; he was advised not to do so but he went by way of fascist Italy. He made it eventually to the south by which time the Allied armies had already landed, and he fought with them back through Italy into France, where he found his parents had been deported to a concentration camp. Again he was told not to do so, but he set off on his own to find them through the ruins of Nazi Germany, soon overrun by the Allies. He found the camp and found evidence, incorrect as it turned out, that his parents were dead. He collapsed onto a bed and it was subsequently claimed that he accidentally blew himself up with a hand grenade he was carrying. Heroism and contingency, a veritable *refus absurde*. His philosophy writing was published posthumously and was much quoted in the course and aftermath of 1968.[3] Evelyne Sullerot was a young resister, who became a distinguished feminist historian and sociologist, who was arrested at age sixteen for "unpatriotic remarks and listening to the BBC." Her father ran a psychiatric clinic in the forest of Compiègne. Her philosophy teacher visited her regularly in prison keeping the concept of liberty alive, and on release she contributed to the hiding of Jews in the clinic; they feigned the madness of the patients when the Germans arrived periodically. She joined a largely student maquis in the Sologne south of Orléans, where she learned much of the early part of René Descartes's *Discours de la méthode* of 1637 by heart; and in 1944 she was caught in the act of burying two maquisards and put up against a wall by a young German soldier to be shot. She kept screaming at him in French which he did not understand. He was unexpectedly called away, and she realized she was free. The contingency is still frightening, even if the philosophy of the absurd is no longer the dominant one it once was among French intellectuals.

Naive, absurd, delinquent, rebellious: these words went into the remaking of the heroic discourse of resistance, and they can still be heard. They suggest a genre of resister which became increasingly related in the 1960s and 1970s not just to existentialist commitment and to contingency, but also to the popular culture of the interwar period when the cultural typologies of the secret agent, the private detective, the spy, and the outlaw captured popular imagination largely through film. What linked these typologies together was their imagined freedom from the levelling forces of mass society presented as a dehumanizing threat by the Spanish sociologist Ortega y Gasset in his book, *The Revolt of the Masses*, in 1929, or by King Vidor in his 1928 film, *The Crowd*, or even earlier in Fritz Lang's 1926 film *Metropolis*. The search, of which these different works were a part, was for a genre of individual who could not be averaged, measured, or restrained by the massification of society, whether social or political. The quixotic, but talented, amateur was a notable form of this genre, exemplified by Richard Hannay in Hitchcock's film of John Buchan's *Thirty Nine Steps* (1935) who embraces illegality and outlaw status in order to unmask the presence of foreign agents. Although often given a delinquent image, the genre fulfilled the alter ego of a society apparently threatened by overregulation and leveling to the point of automation. It plays the role in modern society that Thomas Carlyle gave to "genius," and most romantic writers to "feeling," which raised their heroes above the machine culture of the Industrial Revolution. The typology of the civilian resister as an unusual personality was partially shaped by the continuity of this genre and its spectacular revival in the 1960s, when the threat of consumerism and a one-dimensional society perceived by the New Left on the one hand, and the threat of new ideological extremes perceived by political liberals on the other, took the place of the mass society threat as experienced in the 1920s and 1930s.

In their different and often mutually hostile ways, libertarians and liberals in the 1960s revived the genre of the unorthodox hero or heroine as the defender of freedom. Just as Richard Hannay is recognizable in many 1960s descriptions and self-portraits of SOE agents, so too Emmanuel d'Astier's 1969 depiction of the early resister as a delinquent evoked the cinematic genre of hero in Hitchcock and John Ford, celebrated in the *auteur* (author) theories of the influential film magazine *Les Cahiers du Cinéma*. The ambivalence of the typology was also re-emphasized: many ex-maquisards, for example, began in the 1960s to express their experience of having been treated after the war both as patriotic heroes and also as unregenerate outlaws, to whom jobs or promotion was denied. It became increasingly common for individual resisters to talk about the illegal status which they had voluntarily assumed in their clandestine operations, so that resistance could not easily be interpreted as normative behavior. This relocating of resistance in an unconventional and rebellious mold did almost as much to "break the mirror" in the film *Le Chagrin et la Pitié* as the shift of emphasis toward collaboration. In this respect the words of Emmanuel d'Astier and the portrait of Denis Rake, the SOE agent who talked about his homosexual relationship with a German officer, were as integral to the revision of Occupation history as the discovery and presentation by Marcel Ophuls of the fascist collaborator Christian de la Mazière.

The emphasis on personality declined as research into resistance expanded and developed, and in the late 1980s, its ascendancy began to be reversed. The new discourse, the new codes of resistance history, started to prioritize the context of place and of time, the context of prehistories in the 1930s and well beyond, the context of situations arising from Vichy decisions, or from German initiatives, the context of social and political networks which operate as constraints or possibilities, the context of gender, religion, and race: in short, the history of resistance became subject to the same process of contextualization that prevails in the history of revolutions, wars, syndicalist strikes, or any major political event.

The fact that this is relatively recent might well occasion surprise. Why had historians of the resistance not given such prominence to context before? A few, of course, had. But the discourse of personality had tended to suggest that a convincing sociology of resistance was impossible: the minority and voluntaristic nature of resistance had tended to diminish the importance of context as a determinant. If only a few doctors, politicians, taxi-drivers, midwives, students, peasants, shopkeepers or whatever, resisted, what is the significance of their jobs? If there was a significance why didn't all doctors, politicians, taxi-drivers, midwives resist? The very question "Why some and not others?" took the researcher back to personality.

What changed was this: there was a shift of conceptual awareness occasioned by the more and more frequent use of the term "specificity." One can research the specificity of a profession, of a village or a *quartier* within a town, and reach conclusions about it as a context for resistance activity without getting involved in any generalizations about jobs, countryside, towns, or regions. Discovering the specificity of certain political and social networks in the origin of resistance does not entrain a wholesale politics or sociology of resistance.

The historian has similarly come to use the concept of relativity and to research different and relative chronologies within the resistance. Not everyone in France was affected by the same measures of victimization at the same time: what makes people angry or confident enough to resist may vary from person to person, situation to situation, place to place. Personality is one variable, but only one. Researching the others has preoccupied an increasing number of doctorates, dissertations, monographs, and conference papers. The keywords are specificity and context, particularism and relativity. Personality is there, too, but as one of the specificities.

Take an example from the history of the maquis. The small bands which formed in the woods and hills in the summer and autumn of 1943 were often strengthened by the close relationships with rural communities forged during the long and difficult winter of 1943–4. This was particularly true in the Cévennes, the wooded area of steep valleys and high hills with its sheep rearing, forestry, and mining, just to the northwest of Provence, up above Nîmes and Montpellier, with the coal-mining area of Alès at its center. Why *particularly* true? What are the region's particularisms? Protestantism is one, a puritan culture of Bible and individual responsibility before God: it was the center of the revolt by the Protestant Camisards against Louis XIV and the Catholic establishment at the beginning of the eighteenth century, a revolt which has left its active traditions, its secretive knowledge of caves and mountain paths, and its local pride and defiance. It is a stubborn, hard culture of survival and personal integrity. It is rebarbative, which literally describes the hard, sharp points of the fallen chestnut shells, the stony paths, and the spiky plants which characterize the region, and metaphorically conveys the sharp antagonism of the Cévenols toward authority imposed from outside. In terms of social and economic factors, there is an intimate relationship between the miners in the valleys and the peasant villages in the hills: they are linked by parentage and tradition. Maquisards in the hills needing explosives found it in the stores of the mining companies, and groups of miners would leave their shifts in the evening and go out at night to derail a train with explosives or take food and equipment to the maquis. There was a reciprocity of function and values between town and country. The specificity of the region not only helps to explain why the maquis flourished but also contributes to the very definition of the maquis: not just as a band of men, more or less armed, but as a community of men and women, contriving by various means to liberate whole areas of the countryside from the control of the German army and the Vichy police. In this collective resistance, it would seem that personality played a secondary role. Context and culture were predominant, and they also provide the explanations for the role played by the Cévennes and the neighboring plateau of Vivarais-Lignon in the shelter of Jews, pursued and persecuted by Vichy as well as the Germans. "From infancy, wrote Pastor Bettex, 'I was taught to love the Jews.'" The biblical history of the Jews was widely studied and known, and families took in Jews, resisters, and others on the run without asking questions. It was their religion and culture to give food and shelter to those in need.[4] The historian could easily form a view of the Cévennes as parochial and inner-looking in one sense, but in another it was one of the least xenophobic of French cultures, ready to accept foreigners who were persecuted. In the 1950s they also sheltered members of the Algerian liberation movement, the FLN.

This specificity cannot be used to claim that all Cévenols were resisters, nor to assert that personality was irrelevant, but the clash between a discourse of place and context on the one hand and the discourse of personality and heroism on the other sometimes seems self-evident. In early April 1944 the flamboyant personality of two of the leaders of a maquis unit, known after the Free French victory in North Africa as the Maquis Bir-Hakeim, clashed with the stern prudence of the Cévenol culture. The maquis had started in southwest France; it had moved right across the south: it was mobile and daring in its exploits and carried with it a reputation for youthful bravura which attracted recruits, but it was never rooted in a local community or structure like the majority of the Cévenol maquis. Its leaders Jean Capel, known as Commandant Barot, and Capitaine Demarne, were in many ways exemplars of the talented, outrageous, and heroic adventurer who has entered resistance history as the paradigm personality. Barot spoke excellent German and cavorted with German officers in order to get strategic information: he carried a false identity card as a member of the Vichy police and would demand a respectful salute from Vichy officials. The two drove around the area in a conspicuous black Citroen, stopping and talking to Germans without caution, and the Maquis launched ambushes and attacks on German patrols with little consideration for reprisals on the surrounding communities. These attacks rattled the German command and undermined Vichy authority in the countryside, but their nature ran counter to the tactics of the Cévenol maquisards. Eventually, the stern and cautious particularities of the Cévenol culture forced a showdown, and the Maquis Bir-Hakeim was told to leave the Cévennes. The more anonymous leaders of more anonymous maquis groups had made the decision. Personality was forced to take second place to context. The historiography of resistance in the area has come to reflect this: we now have microstudies of communes and localities as the optimum way into an understanding of resistance.

We are still left with the question of whether Barot's conduct was symptomatic of a particular kind of personality, and if so, whether such a personality was a good qualification for the kind of guerrilla warfare which pitted small bands of poorly armed maquisards against the technological strength of the German army. Those who joined the Maquis Bir-Hakeim because of its reputation for panache, defiantly defend its leaders, but it is worth noting that the successor to Barot and Demarne, when the Maquis settled in the area near Clermont-l'Hérault after heavy losses, was François Rouan. Rouan was a French army officer whose political affinities were a cross between anarchism and Trotskyism; he had deserted to fight for the International Brigades in Spain, had been court-martialled, but was reintegrated as an officer and decorated for his courage, only to desert again to try and join the Free French in 1940. His personality, to judge from these basic facts, would seem to fall within the quixotic and eccentric categories, but as a resistance leader he was famed for his careful and rational approach, his insistence on preparation, and his lack of flamboyance. Personality studies, if they are to enlighten the history of resistance, have to be subtle and nuanced. Rouan himself, in his explanations to me of why resistance thrived in certain areas and not others pointed away from personality toward context and culture. For him the discourse of heroism minimizes the enormous importance of the ordinary, local person in the infrastructure of the resistance.

The new codes, the new discourse, have anchored new categories of resistance in the evolving historiography of Occupied France. Relativity of place, job, time, and person has created a relativity of definition, to the point where it can reasonably be asked whether resistance can be defined outside the context in which it occurs. A military definition of armed struggle against the Occupier, only becomes useful and meaningful in 1943–4. Struggle through words and information, resistance as alternative communication, is much nearer the realities of 1940–2. Struggle through sabotage has to be accepted. Struggle through refuge and aid defines the resistance of thousands who never thought of holding a gun or transmitting a secret code. Resistance as a state of mind which enabled people to respond to a particular crisis or opportunity, perhaps only once when the situation arose has to be considered, too. And what about resistance as silence in the face of police interrogation, or as stubborn survivalism? Can the peasant farmer who withholds goods from either Vichy or the Germans see his or her refusal elevated into resistance? It depends entirely on the context. It makes for endless opportunities for research. Every nuance of every situation calls for careful and full reconstruction before it can be placed in or outside the history of resistance. The discourse of heroism has to be subject to the same contextualization.

Since the mid-1980s the privileged position of the individual resister as hero and heroine has been dislodged surprisingly by the growth of memory studies and the analysis of commemoration. These have combined to foreground national and local sites of memory and produce new conceptual insights into the role of representation in national history and culture. Pierre Nora's pioneer multivolume work, *Les Lieux de Mémoire* ("Sites of Memory") published between 1984 and 1992, has been accepted, not uncritically, as the original source of this new awareness, and it is further accepted that the fortieth and fiftieth anniversaries of events in the Second World War provided much of the content and stimulus necessary to make this awareness into something approaching an academic discipline, or to be more accurate, an interdisciplinary field of study. University courses in memory studies are one indication of this wholesale displacement of event into representation. Public memory is mythopoeic, so that memory, representation, and myth form a powerful intellectual trilogy as keywords in understanding the role of the past as it is recast and exploited in an ever-changing present.

In many ways, however, this scenario is set to be upstaged by an ongoing twist in the approach to resistance. It dates mainly from 1989 and the collapse of communist power. In under ten years there was not only an obvious shift away from Marxism but also a marked decline in the study of revolutions. Comparative resistance studies began to emerge in their place, comparisons between different models of resistance across time and place, such as the resistance of slaves to slave owners, peasants to encroaching landlords, colonized people against imperialist rule, workers' resistance to employers, black resistance to whites in South Africa, and cultural resistance to Stalinist regimes in Eastern Europe. Such comparative studies thrive on the understanding of patterns and rituals of resistance, which the anthropologist James C. Scott called "weapons of the weak," such as foot-dragging, false compliance, dissimulation, jokes, sabotage, small acts of defiance, the kind of action which can remain undetected if undertaken collectively, and which can humiliate as well as undermine authority, resulting in subtle inversions of power, if only in the short term.[5]

This comparative awareness gave a new conceptual edge to the shift in the historiography of French resistance, the shift toward specificity and the foregrounding of context and place. Its most immediate effect was the consolidation of gender-based research into resistance. The shift from gender-ignorant to gender-conscious analysis in France owed much to the feminist input from US and British researchers. Most resistance historians before the mid-1980s took pains to assert that individual women had been among the eminent resisters: Bertie Albrecht, Danielle Casanova, and Lucie Aubrac were names in everyone's list of resistance heroes and heroines. There had been a major conference of women resisters in 1975, *Les femmes dans la Résistance*, initiated by the Communist organization, the Union des Femmes Françaises, and held at the Sorbonne. It was a high point in women's reclamation of their resistance past. But the impact on resistance historiography was slight, and women resisters continued to be treated either as a small number of outstanding heroines or as an anonymous background element in an essentially male story.

The massive shift in conceptualization, consolidated since 1989, has utilized theoretical studies of behavioral patterns and actions which are often shrugged away as natural. What does "natural" mean when used in this sense? Of course, giving shelter or food to those on the run can be called natural. But if it was so natural, why didn't everybody do it? We could be back to personality again, but more pressingly there is the need to question the word "natural" to find out how it has been constituted to eliminate the notion of choice. Men who took to the woods as maquisards never use the word "natural" to describe their action, although it could be argued that it was an atavistic, archetypal, "natural" male pattern of behavior. As "the graffiti artist" of 1968 recognized, the maquisards have a right to insist on the voluntary nature of their actions. But this insistence can no longer be gender-specific. Women's actions under the Occupation are now being reevaluated in terms of the voluntarism which characterized male resistance. Putting the element of choice back into behavior so often described as "natural" has become a research necessity. With it goes an attack on the anonymity of so many women resisters. Names are uncovered and revealed. The discourse of heroism finally began to include ordinary women and choice. So, for example, the edition of *Ouest-France* of May 23–24, 1988, featured Marie Ledier, a village woman of Brullemail in the Orne, who died in 1987. She was posthumously awarded the Israeli honor of *Juste parmi les nations* for hiding Jews in her farm continuously throughout the Occupation. One of the children hidden was André Bornstein aged five in 1942 and now known as Alon Beeri, an Israeli citizen. His citation of Marie Ledier contained the words: "She never asked questions. She viewed it as natural to welcome people and children who had lost their homes and roots." And he concluded: "But she risked her own life to save ours."

The importance of this inclusive move by historians cannot be overstated. But its conceptual strength has a dimension which might be missed if gender inclusion was thought to be its only effect. Its significance lies also in a return to other collective categories, driven as it is by anthropological insights. Pierre Bourdieu's concept of the "habitus," a collective domain of ideas and influences which determine group identity and action, is being widely used to explore the extent to which there was group or community resistance. This strengthens work on local communities who have both a collective habitus and a shared habitat, such as Protestants in the Cévennes, but it also reintroduces a focus on political groupings, so that communists, the losers in 1989, are paradoxically reassessed as a collective force—there is a new interest, too, in class, jobs, and professions, primary schoolteachers, for example. In 1997 the historical establishment in France brought out a book for the first time on the sociology of resistance, with chapters on medics, railway workers, the middle classes, and on women, alongside chapters on theory. Anthropology and sociology thus met up with the specificity and contextuality of historical research.

Was it a permanent swing away from the exceptional and if so how will it affect the discourse of heroism? Do we have any answers? Francis Cammaerts, on any count a hero of SOE, with a personality marked by being a conscientious objector at the start of the war, was far closer to grassroots resistance in the southeast of France than many other allied Agents, and I like the answer which he provided in the title of a modest documentary, made in his area of resistance in 1995. Let me offer his title as a definition of the hero and heroine, which is a democratization of the concept and which allows for most of the shifts and reappraisals in the discourse of heroism that I have tried to present: they were ordinary people, but better still he called them "No Ordinary People."[6]

*   *   *

One of my first interviews was with Romain Baz on May 10, 1969, in Annemasse, a town in the Haute Savoie, bordering Geneva and southern Switzerland. I had been given his name as someone who had been among the very first resisters in the area.

M. Romain BAZ

I was aged thirty in 1940 and was recently married. I was a schoolteacher (*instituteur*) and a militant trade unionist and had been a member of the Socialist Party until 1938. I left the party then because I thought Léon Blum was selling out to the bourgeoisie. I was then politically unattached for a while. I had opposed the Munich agreements because they were obviously in the interests of the bourgeoisie who were preparing for the defeat of France. When it happened in 1940 it was no surprise to me. It had been carefully prepared for years. The ruling classes had betrayed the country.

When the defeat at the front was known, I asked for arms to be distributed to the citizens of Annemasse. My demand was dismissed out of hand by the police, and as soon as the Vichy government was in power I was removed from my job in Annemasse because I was a "danger to the youth of the town." I was sent to a reactionary rural commune at Boëge, some fifteen kilometers due east of Annemasse, and was under strict observance. The result was the opposite of the one intended. I did not change: the rural commune did. It became almost totally a Resistance area.

At the start there was complete resignation among the people. Very few wanted to continue the fight. My wife was a typist and we had typed and distributed our own tracts in Annemasse telling people to be patriots and not to accept the defeat. I was against the Armistice and Pétain right from the start. I suppose my reasons were both patriotic and political. I was utterly scornful of the claim by Pétain that the Armistice had been an honorable event: it was a real swindle. But 90 per cent of the war veterans of 1914–18 joined Pétain's Légion, and although I argued with many of them they usually answered by saying that Pétain knew best how to get the better of the Germans.

The first group we created in the Boëge valley was in the shape of a sports association. It was above suspicion because it had a priest attached to it. The young members distributed tracts and organized listenings to the BBC. The tracts came from Combat, then from the Communist Party and other resistance movements. We distributed everything. Recruitment was steady, but quickest among young people. I'd say that by mid-1942 the Resistance was a popular position even if not always an active one. People had gradually realized that the promises of 1940 had not been fulfilled. For example, the prisoners of war had not come home. France was being exploited by the Germans even if there was no real hunger in the countryside—nothing to compare with Nice or Marseille where people really starved.

I was arrested on the evening of July 14, 1942, while distributing tracts in Annemasse, calling on young workers not to fall for Laval's *Relève* (Relief) scheme and not to go to Germany. I was sentenced to eighteen months' imprisonment for "action harmful to the government and the nation," and was imprisoned first at Annecy, then at Chambéry, then, after fourteen months in a camp from which I escaped and returned to the Boëge valley. At Chambéry I met a lot of communist prisoners, some of whom were under sentence of death. I then joined the Communist Party myself.

In our valley there wasn't much difference between those who joined Combat, Libération, or the communist Front National. Party politics didn't enter into it. There was a saying at the time that if you have to make a pact with the devil to drive out the Germans you choose the devil every time. We used to call ourselves "Les Rouges et les Noirs," because we combined extreme left-wingers with right-wing clericals.

In February 1982 I was in the middle of a year's research, based in Montpellier, and it was near here on February 4 that I visited a married couple, Monsieur and Madame Prades, who had been closely involved with the actions of the maquis group Bir-Hakeim, already referred to in this chapter. Monsieur did most of the talking in the interview, but Madame Prades continuously reminded him of names and facts and provided him with corrections to his story. Frequently they both talked at the same time.

M. and Mme. PRADES

M. PRADES: I was twenty-two in 1942, just married, and we were living at Saint-Saturnin, not far from Clermont-l'Hérault. I'd finished at the École Normale in 1940 and was therefore a schoolteacher (*instituteur*), but because my father was a foreigner Vichy law prevented me from teaching, although

I was born and bred in the locality. I wasn't at all political. I was in the Vichy *Chantiers de la Jeunesse* (Youth camps) in 1941–2, but organized resistance acts like sabotaging the deliveries of wood that were meant for the Germans. In March 1943 I was called up under the Compulsory Labor Service Act (*STO*) but managed to get a postponement until July. They kept coming for me and finally I was compelled to go. My wife packed me a suitcase and I made as if to get the STO train from Montpellier but went to Ganges, on the edge of the Cévennes, instead.

Mme. PRADES: I was from Ganges and knew the mayor. All at the town hall were in the Resistance, all were Protestants, making false identity cards for those "escaping from STO" (*réfractaires*).

M. PRADES: Two of us *réfractaires* went toward le Vigan. Not all the peasants were hospitable. They were frightened, some of them. An old woman refused me a piece of cheese. We got to Aulas where the woman schoolteacher (*institutrice*) directed us to a nearby farm. We knocked at the door. Imagine the scene: they were all seated round the large table, the patriarch, an old woman, and five or six children from very young to aged twenty. The peasant was a veteran of 1914–18 and very patriotic. They sat us at the table for a meal, then lodged us in fresh hay in the barn. We slept for twenty-four hours. Eventually, we made contact with the others in the Mont Aigoual area: we cut wood and made charcoal. In 1944 I was sent to make contact with Bir-Hakeim. I stayed with the maquis, close to the village where my wife was the *institutrice*.

In Bir-Hakeim most were young peasant workers from the region, but there were also those who had fought in the International Brigades in Spain; some came from Paris, others from the Aveyron, Lozère, and everywhere. There were teachers and doctors in the group, too. Demarne and Rouan were the leaders: Demarne was anti-communist, Rouan was a Trotskyist. Demarne was very outgoing, imprudent, and went around with a revolver in his hand. Rouan was very cautious, the epitome of cunning and calculation.

We were hardly ever refused food at this time, the spring and summer of 1944, but we had to requisition from wholesalers. We promised reimbursement at the Liberation. We also requisitioned a bank once, but we never burgled houses. What we did was to go to well-known Vichy or pro-German families and demand things directly from them.

Life in the maquis? Never a dull moment. We were always training or carrying out attacks. We used to mix with the local villagers, so there were no sexual hang-ups. We weren't an isolated maquis in the woods away from everything. The local peasants were mostly left-wing and very sympathetic. Being an outlaw was just right for me. It was an extraordinary feeling.

Mme. PRADES: It was the optimism and hope that was extraordinary.

M. PRADES: I got to the point where the possibility of being killed just wasn't important.

Mme PRADES: And there were such deep friendships.

M. PRADES: I've never known such friendships, right across the political spectrum. Our achievement was to create a climate of insecurity and panic for the Germans. When Demarne was killed the Germans celebrated. We were that important. The women were the liaison agents. They did a terrific job. They looked after all the wounded and provided food and clothes.

Mme PRADES: What the women did was just as dangerous as the actions undertaken by men. Women were often taken as hostages. I myself hid grenades in the empty desks in my classroom. But no search was ever made.[7]

3

The Aubrac Affair

I first met the Aubracs in 1979 when I was compiling two BBC Radio 4 documentaries for the fortieth anniversary of 1940.

I already knew of Lucie as a pioneer resister who had helped form the movement Libération-sud in 1941 and of Raymond as a resister who became Commissaire de la République at the Liberation in Marseille. He had survived arrest and torture when he was captured with Jean Moulin and six other resistance leaders at Caluire, outside Lyon, on June 21, 1943. He was held by Klaus Barbie, the infamous Gestapo chief who was known to resisters as the "butcher of Lyon."

In a long interview in 1979 in their Paris flat, I heard at first-hand the story of how Lucie, pregnant with their second child, had organized Raymond's escape by pretending to the Gestapo to be the aristocratic mistress of the imprisoned Raymond and pleading with them to allow Raymond to be brought from prison to the Gestapo offices to marry her so that her child would be legitimate and her honor saved. Raymond's imminent execution was decreed by Barbie, but various other German officials were taken in by Lucie's consummate acting, and they allowed the act of marriage to take place in the Gestapo headquarters on October 21, 1943. Lucie and a group of armed resisters then carried out a minutely planned and successful ambush of the Gestapo lorry taking Raymond back to the prison.

Lucie's astonishing and dramatic story was finally published in full in 1984 as *Ils partiront dans l'ivresse* (Éditions du Seuil), and in its English translation of 1993 as *Outwitting the Gestapo*.

It was made into a TV film in 1991 by Michel Rotman and Josée Yanne titled *Boulevard des hirondelles,* the name of the street in which the ambush of the lorry transporting Raymond and other resistance prisoners took place.

In 1996 Raymond told his side of the story in his memoirs titled *Où la mémoire s'attarde* (Where Memory Lingers) and in the same year Claude Berri made a major film of the event calling it simply *Lucie Aubrac.* It was widely seen in France early in 1997 and opened in Britain a year later. Carole Bouquet played Lucie and Daniel Auteuil was Raymond.

What I want to do in the following pages is not to reconstruct that event, but to show how the story of two civilians and the issues of history, memory, the law, the media, resistance, and the Holocaust are inextricably interwoven.

The international background was the accelerated pace of academic research and media enquiry into the history of the Holocaust, associated in France with the meticulous documentation and detection by Serge Klarsfeld and many other scholars, including the American Robert Paxton and the Canadian Michael Marrus, and firmly located in the public arena by Claude Lanzmann's *Shoah* in 1985 and such widely read books as Claudine Vegh's *Je ne lui ai pas dit au revoir* ("I didn't have time to say goodbye") published in 1979.

Throughout the whole decade of the 1980s, the major area of research carried out by the government-funded Institut d'Histoire du Temps Présent (IHTP) was an in-depth analysis of the Vichy regime, and it was a sign of the growing conflicts within that research that conferences on Vichy were more and more interrupted by demands from young Jewish (and not only Jewish) researchers that the French historical establishment should address the issue of Vichy's responsibility in the Holocaust, and whether or not the resistance was any less guilty.

The second investigation of Paul Touvier, one of the leaders of the Vichy Milice in the Savoie and then in the Rhône, had begun in 1981, while two years before, in 1979, Jean Leguay, a senior Vichy official involved in the roundup of 8,160 Jewish women, men, and children in the Paris Vélodrome d'hiver (Vel' d'hiv') on July 16–17, 1942, was the first French citizen to be charged with crimes against humanity.

The year 1981 also saw the highly controversial media indictment of Maurice Papon in *Le Canard enchaîné* on May 6, but the main person referred to in the heated exchanges in the conferences was Leguay's superior, René Bousquet, who, as head of the Vichy police, played the major French role in the Vel' d'hiv' roundup. Bousquet had been treated lightly in 1949 by a court which decided that his services to the Resistance in 1943–4 were sufficient to act as mitigation for his actions as police chief, which were not seriously investigated. Since then he had escaped any official enquiry, and it was repeatedly asked throughout the 1980s who was protecting him at the highest level if not President Mitterrand himself.

The trial of the German head of the Gestapo in Lyon, Klaus Barbie, who had been brought back from Bolivia in February 1983, opened in May 1987 and gave a new stimulus to the cases against Bousquet, Touvier, Leguay, and Papon. Barbie was convicted, but in 1989 Leguay died before being tried, and on June

8, 1993, Bousquet was assassinated by Christian Didier, an eccentric who had already tried to kill Barbie in 1987.

The assassination occurred three days before Bousquet was to appear before a court which was set to try him for responsibility for the deportation of Jewish children to the death camps.

Less than a year later, in April 1994, after a five-week trial, Paul Touvier was convicted of crimes against humanity. He was not the first French citizen to be accused of such crimes—that was Leguay—but the first to be convicted. By the time of the trial, the IHTP had turned its research energies away from Vichy to a massive research program on "The Resistance and the French" inaugurated in December 1993 in Toulouse in the first of six major international conferences. Within this program, the Aubracs were seen as distinguished representatives of the Resistance. They had been present in the 1980s at various academic events, often as silent listeners rather than participators—for example, they would not be drawn at a conference in 1983 on the role of the Communist Party at the time of the Nazi–Soviet pact, even though this was the first academic occasion when communist and non-communist historians had agreed to meet together on an issue relating to Occupied France and the Resistance, and the Aubracs were in an ideal position to intervene, having been very close to communist resisters throughout the war.

It was the Barbie trial, following shortly after Lucie's memoirs, that propelled the Aubracs into a more expansive mode. Barbie's maverick counsel, maître Jacques Vergès, nurtured a personal contempt for ex-resisters who had supported the French war against Algerian independence, and he claimed that he would use the trial to expose the moral hypocrisy of resistance leaders. Surprisingly he failed to produce any of the revelations he had promised, but in a filmed interview he settled for another tactic to divert attention away from the guilt of his client. He suggested that Raymond and Lucie had quite possibly been the traitors in the drama of Caluire in June 1943 when Jean Moulin had been arrested, and therefore were indirectly responsible for the death of Moulin, which had followed prolonged and brutal torture by Klaus Barbie.

Vergès was immediately accused and convicted of slander, and in revenge he cited Raymond to appear as a witness for his client Barbie, thereby perpetuating the insinuation that there had been a secret deal between the Aubracs and the Gestapo chief. He knew perfectly well that Raymond could not raise this in court as the arrest of Moulin and others at Caluire was not part of the judicial proceedings against Barbie.

Raymond thought of refusing to appear, but finally decided to do so in order to use the opportunity to testify against Barbie on the issue of war crimes against the Jews. He took the witness stand and read out a statement accusing Barbie of the specific deaths of his own parents, both Jews, who had been arrested by the French Milice, handed over to Barbie, and deported to Auschwitz.

In 1990 the imprisoned Barbie, motivated probably by the fact that Raymond had helped identify a photograph of him in South America, and by the knowledge that Lucie Aubrac had outwitted him in 1943, named Raymond as the betrayer of Moulin in a document, known as *Le testament de Barbie*, which was made public after Barbie's death in September 1991.

The testament was immediately denounced by ex-resisters of all political persuasions as the last malicious lie of an unrepentant old Nazi, who had not once mentioned the name of Aubrac during the entire forty-two years between 1943 and his forced return to France, even though he was known to have spoken from South America about the Moulin arrest.

We thus have the Aubracs in 1996 in the following situations:

First: They had both written memoirs, and Lucie had given numerous interviews about her role in Raymond's escape. This story had been made into one feature-length film and the second was about to open on screens across the country with the star billings of Berri, Bouquet, and Auteuil. Lucie had also continued to practice her teaching gifts and skills by talking to lycées about the resistance, women in the resistance, anti-fascism, and related subjects, using a combination of personal memory and historical interpretation. She was invariably lively, stimulating, and forthright in her opinions. Together they tended to look to each other to supplement memory failures or substantiate facts and interpretations. In a film made in Toulouse, they argued about the degree to which resistance had been illegal and what that implied for resistance motivation. It was a riveting exchange which lit up the documentary.

Second: They were increasingly used by historians as prestigious "témoins" (witnesses) in the series of working seminars and conferences at which memory became one of the central issues. They were, in short, the first recourse for the Parisian academic historians who wanted to make a gestural reference to oral testimony, *témoignage*. It is important to note that only a few of the more established Paris-based historians of the Second World War made any rigorous attempt to integrate individual oral memories into their research, and there were often indignant complaints from ex-resisters at the major conferences about the neglect shown by the historical establishment as a whole. The answer from authoritative historians was repeatedly the same: memory does not constitute history; it constitutes representations of history. In answer to that, the most persistent of the *témoins* continued to insist that their memories be treated as significant evidence, and that their presence at conferences be treated with more academic respect. In Toulouse in December 1993 there was a really bitter exchange of views on this issue, but in all such exchanges the Aubracs played a notably reconciliatory role.

Third: As objects of slander by Vergès and incrimination by Barbie, they had emerged successfully from yet another historical battle with the forces of Nazism and Collaboration, a battle which had united notable ex-resisters in a show of impressive unity in defence of the integrity and positive image of the Resistance.

Fourth: Look at the relevant public context: there had just been the Touvier trial; the dossier against Papon was persistently in the news; there was the publication in 1995 of Serge Klarsfeld's most moving *Mémorial*, listing every Jewish child deported from France, accompanied by family photographs; there were the revelations by the investigative journalist, Pierre Péan, of Mitterand's Vichy past and his suspected protection of Bousquet; there was a steady growth of popular support for Le Pen and the racist Front National; and pandering to this racism, there was the Pasqua law of 1995 which removed the automatic right to French citizenship from children born in France of immigrant parents; in this context, the fact that Raymond Aubrac was Jewish and that his parents were victims of the Holocaust gave his resistance memories a particular, added, resonance and immediacy.

The dynamic of these situations quickened with the opening of the Berri film early in 1997. Many of the leading historians involved in the IHTP's series of conferences were dismissive, disappointed, even angry at Berri's failure to produce the kind of factual document on resistance that could have served as a visual reference point for several years of close reconstruction of people and events. In March at Aix-en-Provence where the last of the conferences was held, there were many statements in group conversations that Lucie's story had always been overromanticized and that the Aubracs had somehow overstepped their role, even though they were not at all responsible for the film itself or for the personification in the title.

In the same month, the Aubracs were paid a warm public tribute in a live three-hour television broadcast from Lyon in the popular "Marche du Siècle" ("*March of the Century*") series facing questions from an audience of French and German sixth-formers and their teachers, alongside Elie Wiesel, winner of the Nobel Peace Prize, who represented the personal memory of the Holocaust. The program was subtitled "Un amour dans la résistance" ("A Story of Love in the Resistance"), and extracts from the two feature films of the Aubrac story were shown together with the video recording of Raymond Aubrac's testimony at Barbie's trial which had not been publicly seen before, and an excellent school product from the Languedoc town of Béziers, documenting a trip to meet Lucie Aubrac in her Cévennes house as part of a project on women in the resistance. The reception given to the Aubracs was admiring but also probingly responsive to every detail of their story. Whatever the critical and academic response to Berri's film, it was obvious that the televised image of the Aubracs' resistance was very positive, and Elie Wiesel's elegant, moving miniature of Holocaust memory had now been placed at the center of that image.

Three weeks later the entire reputation and integrity of the Aubracs were challenged by the publication of *Aubrac, Lyon 1943* by a well-known journalist, Gérard Chauvy. In his account of events leading up to and following the arrest of Jean Moulin, Chauvy reproduced a great number of documents, including the whole of Barbie's "Testament" and compared them to the oral and written memories of the Aubracs. His stated aim was to reveal inconsistencies in the story which was currently on screens all over France, and although he stopped short of endorsing Barbie's incrimination of Raymond, the insinuations were such that the reader was invited to question the veracity of the Aubracs and to imagine that Barbie and Vergès might have been right.

There was an immediate public protest by nineteen well-known resisters, including the Jewish resister and historian, Adam Rayski. At the IHTP the book was seriously digested, document by document. One reasoned reaction was to find Chauvy's analysis of the documents deeply flawed and his arguments malicious. Another was to criticize the tendentious way the book was written, to register it as a misleading historical account and yet to conclude that the documents showed that the Aubracs had a number of questions to answer.

Despite the support of fellow ex-resisters, the Aubracs felt that a public opportunity to prove their integrity would be the best way of dealing with Chauvy's damaging insinuations. The daily newspaper *Libération* offered to stage and report a meeting between the Aubracs and a selected group of historians from the IHTP, and several other academics who had been in the Resistance, and on May 17, 1997, this took place. The session lasted over five hours, and two months later *Libération* published the transcript of the entire exchange in a twenty-four-page pullout (July 9, 1997), with an introduction which claimed its singular importance as an event in oral history, giving "an exciting insight into the process of memory and the profession of the historian."

The transcript and the subsequent personal reactions of each participant, published by *Libération* and put onto the internet, record the unanimous opinion of the historians that the Barbie–Vergès "Testament" was a fabrication, and that Chauvy should not have given it any semblance of credibility. The Aubracs did not betray Jean Moulin.

But beyond this clear statement, the *Libération* transcript was such an ambiguous publication that it suggested that this so-called discussion should, in reality, be called "the Aubrac trial." What was conceptualized as a public way of vindicating the two venerable resisters, in fact, turned into a tense quasi-judicial process, in which some of the IHTP historians blurred the distinctions between research questioning and interrogation, and assumed all three roles of interrogator, judge, and jury. They criticized Lucie for embellishments and a tendency to mythification, and Raymond for inconsistencies in his recall of dates and in his use since the war of the various pseudonyms which had cloaked his real identity as Raymond Samuel. These criticisms were not without some foundation, but the moral sermonizing about truth which accompanied them seemed to be excessively judgmental. Still further it was little short of astonishing to see Daniel Cordier, the resistance secretary and rightly admired biographer of Jean Moulin, venture the possibility that carelessness of the Aubracs in attention to detail might indicate failures in their cover and security in 1943, which might explain the arrest not of Jean Moulin but of Raymond's mother and father. Unsurprisingly, it was this that prompted Raymond's most critical reaction to the whole event. He wrote,

> I hardly dare mention the hypothesis, formulated for the first time by Daniel Cordier, according to which Lucie and I might bear an indirect responsibility for the arrest of my parents, arrested at the end of November 1943 as Jews, transferred to Drancy, and gassed on their arrival at Auschwitz. It is, however, fully established that they were the victims of the round-up of Jews by the Nazis and their auxiliaries in the French Milice. . . . The insinuation which had nothing to do with the rest of the discussion, has deeply wounded me. Are the survivors guilty?

Much of the emotion within the question, if not the question itself, was directed at historians, so it is necessary therefore to list a few of the ways in which the Aubrac Affair still promotes a serious analysis of the relationship of historians to the issue of memory.

In the first place, the context in which memories are given is readily problematized by historians, but the context in which memories are received, used, and reused, must be analyzed by historians with more critical self-awareness. In 1996 the Aubracs were still a prestigious presence at academic seminars, their oral and written accounts neither doubted nor investigated. And yet, only a year later when the IHTP historians took part in the *Libération* event, it was surely immensely significant that Claude Berri's film was seen by some of them as a romanticization, making them embarrassed about the Aubrac story, and keen to distance themselves from it. Chauvy's documents were not new to the historians, nor were the Aubracs' memories. What was unexpected was the virulence with which personal memory was now chastised as unreliable.

Second, the prolonged presence of the judicial dossiers, trials, and detection relating to Leguay, Bousquet, Papon, Touvier, and Barbie, heightened the burden of proof which lies at the heart of archival, historical work. Memory was not accepted as proof enough—hence the constant tendency to locate memory as representation, shading into memory as mythification, or media-conscious commemoration, the very stuff of Pierra Nora's *Lieux de mémoire* (Realms of Memory). Nora's groundbreaking series of publications in the late 1980s had excitingly prioritized public and national memory, but it made it difficult to know what to do with individual memories. They tended to be seen as inferior, or even inadmissible, in the hierarchy of factual sources, and were frequently arraigned for falsity and invention. This double standard accounts for why individual resisters felt so confused and neglected at the academic conferences on memory and resistance.

Third, there was the centrality of the Holocaust to all research and remembering of the Vichy period. This was evidenced in the presence of Elie Wiesel at the TV program on the Aubracs, and in the hypothesis of a possible responsibility linking the Aubracs to the arrest of Raymond's parents, which arose as if from nowhere in the *Libération* event. There was an acute awareness of the issues of rationalization about Holocaust responsibility, or denial. The dominant mode of the media is investigative, looking for history that has been hidden: certain historians were concerned not to lose the initiative in this investigative process, which may well explain their virulent interrogation of the Aubracs, and certainly explains their sermonizing about truth, which other historians repudiated after the publication of the *Libération* event, one of them describing it as a "deplorable lesson of history."[1]

This has led directly to the question of who controls the history of the Occupation period, and of the Holocaust? The actors who were there and their memory? The historians? The media? The law? The answer is: they all do, in a constant shifting kaleidoscope of power relations.

The stakes are high. Individual, group, and national reputations are made and broken. The highest moral criteria are in play. It is not only a question of right or wrong but also one of use and misuse.

It is my contention that the Aubrac Affair allowed some historians to assume a position of preeminence which may well lead to hubris. Historians are now hydra-headed. Increasingly they are forensic in the sense of being detectives and investigators into the past. They vie with the law and the media in establishing who did what and when. And they are closest to one of the crucial locations of power: the archives. There has rarely been a period in French history when the status of the professional historian has been so high, when historians become media and courtroom stars. The media and the law both need access to the archives: the expert giving this access is the historian. The media and the law expect the historians to have the answers. They become prime witnesses. Historians decide not just how and why memory is influential: they feel they have also to judge whether it is true or false. The law and the media expect it of them. Have they come to expect it of themselves?

In addition, the historian appears to be expected to take on the role of the shaman, the spirit medium, the raiser and guardian of the dead, the voice of the past. Surely that is precisely the role which historians have normally, and rightly, ascribed to storytellers at the evening veillées (gatherings) round the fire or over a glass of wine at the café. Learning from anthropologists like David Lan we know that oral transmission of the past to the present and the future happens everywhere with or without the presence of the historian. Storytellers transmit the representations of the past which continually form attitudes and opinions and influence actions. It is they who are the spirit mediums. Why usurp their role?[2]

We have to realize that oral memories can supply exactly the personal material historians need to understand the experience of the past, the workings of representation, the power of images and previous histories, the oscillation in attitudes between continuity and change. At the very least, oral memories can provide historians with new hypotheses to work on, and new perspectives to develop. Where this is widely acknowledged, there is an agreed academic approach to the study of memory and the role of oral history. With more than a passing nod to Schiller, testimony does have a specific place in history, but it doesn't, alone, add up to it.

So when the BBC rang up and asked me on a live program whether or not the Aubracs were inventing their past, did I say, "Well, memories provide us with valuable evidence, but no oral testimony, alone, adds up to history"? No, I didn't. I just replied, "No. They are not inventing."

It was a verdict. But a verdict of what? The terrible fact, which I cannot accept, is that the presenter then added: "There we are: there is the verdict of history." It was not, of course, anything of the sort. But I was conscious at that moment of being a judge. In the realm of memory, the Second World War, and the Holocaust, the responsibility is awesome.

4

The Discourse of Exile

At 6:00 p.m. on June 18, 1940, the *SS Madura* sailed from Bordeaux and two days later reached the Cornish coast. "For nearly a whole day," wrote that brilliant journalist Alexander Werth, "we lay anchored in the bay of Falmouth. . . . At last we were taken off. It only then occurred to me that we were *news*, quite big *news* . . . the whole town had assembled to greet us. We were *refugees*."[1]

Three months later, his diary of the last days of Paris was published, one of the first books in what became an opulence of wartime writings about France, published in Britain. They have their own specific history, as does the Francophile community in Britain who eagerly bought and subsidized the diaries, poems, essays, critical commentaries, and personal reminiscences which jostled with the journal *La France Libre* to represent "the soul of France." This dedicated pursuit of the timeless essence of Frenchness produced a flowering of French typologies which have rarely been presented with such an absence of parody and pastiche. In 1945 John Weightman translated a selection of articles from *La France Libre* and published them as *French Writing on English Soil*, with a short introduction which contains the words:

> The French are an exceptionally articulate people, but owing to material difficulties, they have not yet been able to give full expression to the thoughts and impressions they have had during the last few years. What we have here are the first accounts of French mentality during the war, such as they were written by Frenchmen in or out of France, in an atmosphere of exile or under stress of German occupation.[2]

The collection is presented as a composite discourse; it is not fractured by any mention of the dates on which the articles were written, nor by any emphasis on the status, age, gender, or ethnicity of the writers. There is no development within it, only changing subject matter and style, and the distinctive preoccupation and personality of each essayist. The picturesque lies alongside the painfully reflective, the idyll of a mountain village alongside the brutalizing execution of a traitor. It is a rich primary source, not only of the exiles' state of mind but also of what sympathizers in the country of exile expected "the discourse of exile" to be.

If we are to calibrate the place of exile in the history of resistance, we need first to register the huge range of contemporary research into the phenomenon of exile. An explosion of texts and oral evidence on all aspects of exile in the twentieth century—on refugees, the right of asylum, immigrants, ports, frontiers, frontier communities, dual nationalities, international organizations and human rights—has created a "discourse of exile" and has encouraged a thematic genre of resistance studies which is neither time- nor place-specific and which owes much to the anthropology of social and cultural resistance among slaves, the peasantry, and other subaltern classes, which James C. Scott has called "the weapons of the weak."

War and armed struggle, the first thematic grouping in which resistance was situated, is now only one among many contiguous areas of research and theory within which we can formulate new questions about resistance. In so doing we are finally responding to the polyvalence of war. Clearly, one factor above all in the last twenty years has forced us to rethink resistance: the challenge of Holocaust studies. Where once the end product of resistance was judged almost solely as liberation, we now have to evaluate it also in terms of survival. War as displacement, victimization, and exclusion has become as central to the study of the Second World War as war seen in terms of conquest, occupation, and liberation. Resistance is correspondingly redefined.

Most of the new work over the last twenty years has been not on the exiles in London but on the exiles within France: the tens of thousands of Spanish Republican exiles still interned in the southwest of France, the hundreds of displaced Alsace-Lorrainers who sought some way of remaining south of the demarcation line, the anti-fascist and Jewish refugees from Central and Eastern Europe, and the trainloads of Rhineland Jews dumped overnight on October 22, 1940, in the southern zone by Nazi Germany still intent at that stage on expulsion. There is widespread interest in the Guérilleros espagnols (Spanish Guerilla Fighters), in the Jewish and Communist exiles within the MOI (Main d'Oeuvre Immigrée, Immigrant Workers Organization), and in the Italian political exiles, whether in the southeast or the southwest. In the Lot-et-Garonne, for example, the names of Oreste Ferrari and Campolonghi and the newspaper L'Attesa (Expectation) had stood since the 1920s for international resistance against Mussolini, and, in 1943–4, these Italian exiles, mostly tenant farmers, provided a chain of safe houses for Yvonne Cormeau, radio operator with George Starr of the SOE.

There is much still to be discovered on the specifics of resistance by these exiles from other countries, but the subject has been transformed by the research of Jean-Marie Guillon, Robert Mencherini, Geneviève Dreyfus-Armand, Emile Temime, Stéphane Courtois, Denis Peschanski, Adam Rayski, Annette Wieviorka, François Marcot, and many others, and its significance widely acknowledged, and reaffirmed, as in Robert Gildea's chapter "The Blood of Others" in his *Fighters in the Shadows*. The shift of emphasis could be said to have answered the accusation of neglect prompted by the reaction to Mosco's film on the Manouchian affair, *Des "terroristes" à la retraite* ("'Terrorists' in retirement"), first shown on French television in 1985. The intensive research has expanded an area pioneered by Claude Lévy, and once largely occupied by individual Jewish and Communist historians, by Spanish émigré groups, and by anarchist archives such as the CIRA in Marseille, all marginalized for many years after the war by mainstream resistance research. This marginalization has ended. For example, the major conference of 1985 on "La Résistance juive en France" brought Jewish resistance from the margins to the center, after which there has been an acute debate on the definition of Jewish resistance and on the place within it not only of the communist Immigrant Workers Organization (MOI) but also of the Jewish relief organizations, notably the aid to children, the Oeuvre de secours aux enfants (OSE).

This development in resistance historiography has been dramatic. As the Besançon conference of 1992 on "Les étrangers dans la Résistance en France" made clear, it is the wording of "the Resistance in France" rather than "the French Resistance" which allows a forceful representation of the foreign origins and heteroclite histories of those who defied the Nazis and their allies within mainland France. They were integral to both the successes and failures of resistance.

Both a cause and effect of this development has been the inclusion in resistance history of those who responded to the predicament of refugees and those on the run. This enlarged the "discourse of exile" to encompass the ideas, actions, and motivations of those who sheltered and aided the exiles.

In 1985, Michel Goubet and Paul Debauges revealingly set up their account of resistance in the Haute-Garonne with two subsections titled "Un brassage de populations" ("The Intermixture of Peoples") and "L'aide aux réfugiés." They mention the groups who responded to the plight of Spanish Republican refugees in 1939 and add: "It is interesting to note that you find it is the same groups who become involved in aid to German anti-nazis and Jews when they, in turn, are hunted and on the run."[3]

For many years now this has been familiar territory for the historian, particularly since the 1987 book on the Cévennes, *Terre de refuge*, the 1990 conference *Accueil et Résistance* ("Welcome and Resistance") devoted to the plateau Vivarais-Lignon, and the series of major international conferences on the Resistance inaugurated by Jean-Marie Guillon and Pierre Laborie in December 1993 in Toulouse. Numerous studies, some before, but many since, have emphasized the links between aid to the refugees and resistance activity, and whether we start with Françoise Meifredy in Lyon, already mentioned in Chapter 1, or in Brive with Edmond Michelet's reception of Dietrich von Hildebrand and thirteen other refugees sent by Monsignor de Solages from Toulouse, or with the work in Vichy's internment camps of Madeleine Barot, the Polish abbé Glasberg, and the evacuee and refugee organization known as the CIMADE, there is ample documentation to show that humanitarian resistance should not be dissociated from other nascent opposition and resistance activity in 1940–1.[4]

The case of Françoise Meifredy points to the ambiguous political situation of many of those closely involved with prisoners of war who felt that Pétain was an icon of humanitarian leadership. Her meeting with him in May 1941, related in her notebooks, did everything to confirm her loyalty to him in person. It did not stop her from acts of defiant commitment, or protect her from arrest. The telling study published in 2010 of help given to escaping colonial prisoners of war by volunteers such as Meifredy and many social workers is rightly subtitled "Forgotten faces of occupied France" by its author Armelle Mabon. It had been well known that this activity by the retired colonel Hauet and Germaine Tillion, under the banner of a reanimated national union of colonial combatants, led to clandestine involvement with the early Parisian resistance centered on the Musée de l'Homme. Other similar story lines, with or without ambiguity, are there, in Mabon's words, for the first time.[5] There is now more academic interest in lines of escape for prisoners, refugees, and exiles than there probably has ever been. It has had to confront the frequent criticism that flight and escape involved self-interest and avoidance of struggle as well as commitment to resistance. Robert Mencherini raised this issue in his paper on refugee artists and intellectuals in the south, given at the Brussels conference of November 1994. Éveline and Yvan Brès had discussed it in 1987 at the start of their book on German anti-fascists in the Cévennes. Exiles in London, conscious of their relative safety, raised it in the pages of La France Libre. In all of these there is the insistence that flight was usually to resistance of some kind elsewhere. Statistically, we need to know if this is accurate: new research into the ambiguity of flight is still required. The problems encountered will be largely ones of definition, but en route it will widen still further the inclusive search for those who provided the escape and enabled refugees and exiles to survive, whatever the motivation of the helpers and whatever the survivors did as a result.

There is always more to be discovered about the réseaux d'évasion (escape networks) and more informal filières (lines of escape), which originally fell in the terrain of military resistance, but are now reanimated by "the discourse of exile." I received a call from BBC Scotland in 2000 about Donald Caskie. The telephone voice told me that he had died in 1983, and then added, "You know, the eminent Scottish resister in occupied France." There was a slightly embarrassed silence, at both ends of the telephone, before the voice continued, "Well, perhaps not so eminent, since nobody appears to know anything about him, apart from his own book."

I then remembered buying a secondhand copy of *The Tartan Pimpernel* by Donald Caskie for a shilling in 1961. I rediscovered it only after the phone call, and then re-read his highly religious account of being caught up in the *exode* of June 1940 which led him first to Bayonne and then, "by divine guidance" he claims, to Marseille. There, as a displaced person himself he reopened the Seamen's Mission in the rue Forbin in the Vieux Port to help other similar refugees. The mission itself was not clandestine at the start but its purpose soon was:

"I threw open the doors of the Seamen's Mission with a flourish," he wrote in 1957. "Almost immediately, travel-weary visitors began to arrive. . . . Gaunt, sick from exposure, unshaven and ragged . . . marked men, aliens . . . sought by the police who would intern them like animals. . . . We set out to get our house in order as an escape hatch for allied soldiers, airmen and sailors."[6]

Escape lines (*filières*) were created to Toulouse and on to Spain, and in the spring of 1941, Caskie was arrested and interrogated by Vichy police in Fort St Nicholas. The interrogators, he wrote, "were in a difficult position. Every Christian church and convent in Marseille had contact with foreign countries." He was sentenced to two years' imprisonment *avec sursis* (suspended sentence), which is quite innocently rendered in the book, even in the subsequent paperback, as *avec souris* (with mice), a prescient misspelling.

Told to leave Marseille, Caskie was eventually imprisoned first in Grenoble, then at St. Remo in Italy before being taken to Fresnes, the notorious German prison south of Paris. In Paris itself, at the rue des Saussaies, the Gestapo accused him of being an ally of the Jews and condemned him to death, but he survived due to the intervention of a German pastor. His whole account is of an energetic, charitable, and deeply religious man, exile, victim, and resister. The chapter headed "The Feast of the Passover" gives details of his close working with a Jewish family outside Grenoble, the home of Harris Rudowitch and his father-in-law Abraham Korn. Here was a Jewish family who took in and sheltered refugees.

Caskie's close links with the SOE escape network of Pat O'Leary, *nom de guerre* of the Belgian army doctor Albert Guérisse, brings him within the canon of known resistance activity, but otherwise his life and actions are sui generis, except that they weave one of the multiple strands of exile and resistance, refugees and humanitarianism.

Across the Vieux Port in Marseille was the Centre Américain de Secours (*American Aid*) in the rue Grignan, the refuge and escape center animated by the American, Varian Fry. He had arrived there in August 1940 with $2000 and a list of 200 names of endangered European, mainly Jewish, intellectuals and artists, whom the New York Emergency Rescue Committee had decided should be rescued from German persecution and Vichy surveillance, a decision which is still variously described as humanitarian, political, or as the traditional US interest in attracting talent. As Jean-Marie Guillon reminds us, Fry's memoir published in the United States in 1945, *Surrender on Demand*, was not translated into French and remained virtually unknown until the mid-1980s when the memoirs of Daniel Bénédite, one of Fry's main French associates who continued his work among artists at the Villa Air-Bel in the suburbs of Marseille, were published.

Since then, the explosion of academic and media interest in exile and resistance, to which I have referred, has increasingly shifted the hub of research. The mounting knowledge about Fry and his artists came to a climax in the conference of March 1999 in Marseille. In the conference papers we have a multitude of angles and approaches, details and photographs, which document what Robert Mencherini called a "prehistory" of resistance, or in Jean-Marie Guillon's phrase, "resistance before the Resistance." The terms might equally apply to the activity of Caskie's Mission close by. Fry did not refer to him personally but he did point out that by the autumn of 1941 the Unitarian Service Committee had saved 226 refugees, the majority of them Protestant. The Unitarians worked closely with the Emergency Rescue Committee and from the evidence of Jean Gemähling comes an endorsement of Caskie's tribute to Catholic convents in Marseille, which Gemähling credits with acts of charity toward the Jewish refugees.[7]

Acts of humanitarian aid to refugees in 1940–1 did not, however, conform to a single pattern. The range of motivation and goals suggests that the historian of resistance has to be careful not to cluster them all into a generic category of action. In statistical terms, by far the greatest volume of care for refugees had been the municipal provision for the millions who fled in the massive *exode* of May–June 1940 from Belgium and northern France to escape the invading Germans. The reception centers south of the Loire, the thousands of providers of food and shelter, and the local notables who rose to the occasion with leadership and money were all considered an integral part of the moral adulation for the leadership of Marshal Pétain, which swept the country.

Undoubtedly, the temporary exile of millions in the *exode* of 1940 has been the starting point for many studies of both Vichy and the Resistance. The difficulty of categorizing humanitarian action in the first two years of the Occupation has particularly affected the history of Jewish relief organizations. Adam Rayski has rendered the problem concisely: "In the Vichy zone, charitable organisations felt they could not give up the legal existence allowed to them by the Vichy regime, even if it was a limited one. The result was an ambiguous situation for humanitarian bodies which tried to ease Jewish suffering which was clearly caused by the very regime itself."[8] It is precisely when faced with such ambiguity that historians of the resistance also face the difficulty of using the concept of "interior exile" (exil intérieur), one of the structural elements of "the discourse of exile."

The term exil intérieur is used as a subtitle by Laurent Jeanpierre in his contribution to the conference on Varian Fry. It heads a section in which he describes Varian Fry's predicament when he became subject after the war to investigation by the anti-communist Un-American Activities Committee in 1951: "Saviour of undesirables he was condemned to be an undesirable himself, not a martyr but, in the profoundest sense of the word . . . an outlaw."[9]

It is clear that the millions of refugees in the exode of 1940 were not stigmatized as "undesirables" in the sense used by Jeanpierre. But the Jewish refugees saved by Fry undoubtedly were. It follows that something more than geographical displacement within one's own country is needed if the term "exil intérieur" is to have any useful historical meaning for the historian of resistance. It has to indicate a state of social exclusion or of illegality, whether forced or voluntary.

Resisters who give an image of themselves as "uncompromised" usually tie it to an existential sense of displacement. Were they internal exiles in any meaningful sense of the term? Many of their answers in oral testimony have been a proud or wistful "yes" and many claim to have felt the exile more acutely after the war. From others there is no more than a grudging recognition that the term exil intérieur is acceptable only as an overblown synonym for the isolation and raw experience of being different. Jean-Pierre Chabrol in the Cévennes not only celebrated the number of political exiles from Spain and central Europe who made up his maquis grouping of the FTP, but he was also conscious that, as he looked down on the town of Alès he felt he was "on another planet, isolated. . . . Up in the hills we didn't really exist. We didn't really count."[10]

Much of the theoretical work on exile points unsurprisingly to the liminality of the exile, a state of continuous uncertainty and problematic identity. Tzvetan Todorov in L'Homme dépaysé (Disorientated Man) sees it as full of positive possibilities which do not have to lead to acculturation but could result in transculturation, exploring the potential of choice.[11] In the new writing on exile and resistance it is this breaking out and the crossing of frontiers that is prioritized, whether by exiles themselves or those who responded to their predicament. The "other planet" metaphor of Jean-Pierre Chabrol and the "exil intérieur" ascribed to Varian Fry, are merely two from a vast resource of expressions which resisters and their historians have used to emphasize the positive liminality of both exile and resistance, concluding that freedom lay precisely in the "spaces on the borders of authority."

All this produces an interest in a notional "long resistance" of the twentieth century, from anti-fascists in the interwar years, through the networks of support for political refugees in the 1930s, the refusals which created resistance in the Second World War, the anti-torture campaign of the 1950s, the rejection of Stalinism, resistance to racism, and the defense of human rights. It provides a counterbalance to the weight of tyranny and inhumanity seen by many as the dominant narrative of the century.

Even as the discourse of exile encompasses the achievements of humanitarian resistance it runs into the numerous failures of rescue and the negative facts of liminality. I received a specific telephone call about escape a few years ago. A man whose German-Jewish father was deported from France and died in Auschwitz had found his father's last letter dated June 17, 1942, saying that he was with the 318th company of Travailleurs étrangers (*foreign workers*) in Lagrasse in the Aude. What, the son wanted to know, had happened in Lagrasse? I suggested avenues of research, which revealed that the Jews of the 318th company had been put onto the 5th convoy to the French internment camp Drancy, as documented by Serge Klarsfeld. But not all refugee Jews in Lagrasse were seized. Jean Séguy, mayor in 1995, detailed the refuge provided by several families in the commune, notably his own parents and the baker Lucien Bertrand and his wife Agnès Bertrand who was honored by Israel in 1971. The research stopped there. Local questions which the son raised remain: why were some Jews in the Vichy zone sheltered and not others? Were the acts of refuge the work of resistance groupings? If so where were these groups when the 5th convoy was able to leave in August 1942?

These are not new questions, far from it. But they have become more insistent and more specific as the local details of refuge and humanitarianism are increasingly claimed for the history of resistance. Freedom on the borders of authority was created by, and for, very few. The two volumes on Varian Fry underline just how many candidates for emigration had to be refused by American Aid. Could more have been accepted? Was there really a recurrent relationship between exile and resistance in France, or only an occasional one? Once humanitarianism is brought within the compass of resistance we have to assert not only that resistance was a minority phenomenon, but also that so too was humanitarian action.

Equally vital within this generic area, but as yet little studied, is the discourse of "return," probably the main ingredient of the exilic discourse itself.

The third article in *French Writing on English Soil* is by L. de Villefosse, a naval officer in the Free French, who writes:

Naturally, like all sailors, I have lived a good deal outside France, sometimes very far away. And I must confess I never regretted leaving my country. . . . I never looked behind but always forward . . . and whenever I came back . . . I had a feeling of disillusionment. . . . In short the word "exile" had no meaning for me.

But his essay is called "Homesickness," originally a lecture titled "Nostalgie de la France" given on November 14, 1941, at the Oxford University French Club. He goes on to ask, "How is it that I am now intensely conscious of a feeling of exile? Why is it that I miss France?" His answer revolves round the impact of photographs cut out from *La France Libre*,

astonishing photographs which I found occupying a place of honour in many . . . houses around the African coast. For example the towers of Notre Dame on a wintry day, looming above the second-hand bookstalls on the quayside . . . a window opened onto the countryside . . . a quiet river winding along a meadow . . . two stone arches.[12]

We should take these clichéd images seriously. The photographs in *La France Libre*, many by the celebrated photographer Thérèse Bonney, construct a powerful vision of the country to which the exile wants to return: they are obviously an iconography of longing, of homesickness (*mal du pays*) but they are also one of essentialism, defining the nature of the home country by reference to the past and in contrast with the present. "*Autrefois . . .*" ("Once . . .") is the caption beneath a photograph of well-kept telephone lines against the sky; "*Aujourd'hui . . .*" ("Now . . .") has telephone lines in a sagging state of collapse. The issue of January 15, 1943, has four pages of photographs subtitled "We will find once again our river . . . our cottage . . . our little son . . . and our elderly parents." *Retrouver* (find again, rediscover) is the dynamic of this discourse of return.

Gaullist resistance revealed the essence of France to de Villefosse. In his exilic writing there is all the excitement of the new and the unknown which Todorov would approve, but it is accompanied by an essentialist portrait of France as the timeless face of the past to which he is confident France will return. Stripped of its uncomfortable party politics this is exactly how de Gaulle represented the unbroken Republic to which he laid claim in August 1944. But was it just a Gaullist perspective? The dominantly communist FTP maquis revealed the essence of the Cévennes to Jean-Pierre Chabrol. Was this a breaking of frontiers or the reinvention of old ones? After the war, huge numbers of resisters who may be said to have experienced interior exile were content to rediscover societal patterns which were comfortable and familiar. In 1945 the idea of an innovative postwar politics of resistance was stillborn.

Women who had crossed gender frontiers in the resistance point to the ways in which there was a return to conventional male discourse at the Liberation and a subsequent invisibility of women in resistance history. Yet they also acknowledge that they themselves often settled back into familiar and familial roles. Despite the fact that much resistance centered on human rights and the worth of others, the racial hierarchies of prewar colonialism were not discarded after the war but were reimagined as part of an essentialist *France d'outre-mer* (France Overseas), the photographs of a white Notre Dame and a grey Paris assuming an imperial prominence in colonial houses around the African coast.

Given that such a significant proportion of active resisters in France were immigrants and exiles, we should interrogate closely the reasons why the nationality legislation of October 19, 1945, reproduced categories from the 1930s, and in many ways hardened the criteria for naturalization. Essentialist prescriptions exude from this legislation. It is something that Gérard Noiriel has emphasized in his *Origines républicaines de Vichy*, as also Karen Adler in her doctoral research on gender and race between 1942 and 1948, with its heuristic title, "Idealizing France."[13] They both underline the explicit place of regressive assimilationist policy in the immediate postwar context.

There were, of course, insistent demands from many resisters for France to move forwards and for sweeping reforms at the Liberation. Mostly the product of the 1944 radical Charter of the CNR, some of these were met, but many of the expected social changes did not occur until over twenty years later. It was not until the end of the 1950s, writes Noiriel, that the stereotypes underpinning postwar attitudes to nationality, began slowly to give way to "a new, more universalist vision of the world."[14] The theme of exile and resistance, with its discourse of return, foregrounds the extent to which the resistance was transgressive, yet also nostalgic, how it looked toward liberation but also restoration, how it created new identities, and yet reinvigorated old ones.

It takes us by a new path to the paradox of frontiers broken and frontiers re-established. The prevalence of those reestablished after the war obscures for almost two decades the nature of those that had been broken. Foreign names of exiles and refugees in the resistance disappear; military and political modes of resistance obscure civil and cultural forms; the center and the top occlude the periphery and the bottom. A strong element of Jacobin centralism is reaffirmed. Georges Bidault, once the head of the CNR but fully identified with the war against Algerian independence, is in power; Claude Bourdet from Combat and the MUR and one of the first to condemn French torture in Algeria, is not.

What I am trying to say is that first, new approaches to resistance are both cause and effect of a massive shift of emphasis toward refugees and the issues of racism and human rights; second, that these approaches raise the challenging concept of interior exile; third, that the theme of exile and resistance must involve itself with the evidence of failure; and finally, that many of the paradoxes of resistance and its postwar history can be accessed through the discourse of return. We need to know far more about this discourse not only among the London exiles but also within France.

"What remains of our loves . . . a little village, an old clocktower . . . the dear face of my past," sang Charles Trenet during the war. "*Que reste-t-il de nos amours . . . un p'tit village, un vieux clocher . . . le cher visage de mon passé . . . .*" The essentialism here can still bring tears. But what happened, postwar, to many of the liminal "spaces of freedom on the borders of authority"?

*   *   *

My interview with Jean-Pierre Chabrol on March 2, 1982, at his rambling home at Génolhac in the Cévennes was not easy to record. He was surrounded as he spoke by children, running in and out, and various family adults, and was impatient to take me to see his motorbike collection in the outlying barns, which included his prize possession, a German bike with sidecar which he had seized on one of the maquis encounters with German troops. I was aware of his literary persona as the author of novels and short stories set in the local area and had already read the best known, Un Homme de Trop (*One Man Too Many*), *published by Gallimard in 1958.*

M. Jean-Pierre CHABROL

I first made contact with resistance groups in the Sorbonne. I was at a lycée in Paris, aged fifteen in 1940. The German police came looking for me so I went back to my family home in the Cévennes. In the spring of 1944 I decided to join a maquis. I was a Gaullist with expectations of finding a kind of regular army. By mistake I found myself in a maquis FTP formed of miners, peasants, and old members of the International Brigades—Spaniards, Italians, and Poles. I wanted to leave at once. They said, "Do you want to change camp?" I said, "Yes." I only found out later that meant you would be killed. They were very tough. Luckily for me a communist official recognized me and said, "He's alright. He's the son of the *instituteur:* he's a bit of an idiot, but OK." I stayed. It became my reeducation, a new life.

Peasants gave us food. And we carried out raids; for example, when we knew the Germans were about to take a flock of sheep, we raided the sheepfold, tied up the shepherd, beat him up a bit to make it look genuine, and took the animals. Every day there would be some sort of action. Miners would come from the day shifts in Alès to help us at night. Then they would go back to work. We would walk 10 to 12 kilometers for some sort of action, then back again the same night. And there was night duty, some way from the camp.

We weren't really afraid of the dark, but it was easy to get lost. But there were strange noises. A hedgehog in the dead leaves: it farts, it breathes, it snores just like a man. At dusk or at dawn I would see smoke coming up from Alès. I felt as if I were on another planet, isolated. I imagined life down there, people going to the cinema, making love, eating, listening to the radio. Surely they had forgotten us. The war seemed to go on and on. I thought it would never end. And here we were; we didn't really exist. We didn't really count.

But when we went down to the villages we were welcomed with tears and kisses. There was no question of peasant hostility. Miners were all from peasant families. And even foreigners down the mine are part of a fraternity.

In my first maquis up in the Bougès mountain we went on an operation along exactly the same paths as the Camisards had used in the early eighteenth century. I found this out only fifteen years later. At the time I knew little about the Camisards, nor about Karl Marx. For Protestants, the outlaw and the exile were sacred. Later on they hid Ben Bella and other FLN members during the Algerian War.

I'm not sure if I enjoyed being an outlaw. There were moments of happiness, but I also suffered a lot. The maquis meant everything to me. There was no democracy. You obeyed orders. Equality, yes. All had the same rights. There was a sort of savagery, being young. You killed with a kind of joy. Death meant nothing.

The Liberation meant going home. Everyone mobbed us in the villages. Women had been vital as liaison agents. A girl called Gilberte, aged sixteen, sent us information about German troop movements, all written by hand. It was very useful. She was deported to Ravensbrück but survived. I met a young woman after the war and talked to her about the maquis and the important note we had received, and she said, "Gilberte, that's me."[15]

5

The Specificity of Place

Somehow I always accepted that I would end up debating an aspect of General de Gaulle with Douglas Johnson, professor of Modern French History at the University of London.[1] Our discussions had that implicit understanding ever since our first meeting in the early 1970s. It wasn't a pact, more a mutual sense of the inevitable: like a repeated ramble along a familiar street when sooner or later we would come to the same distinctive monument which demanded that we stop and look. Depending on light, weather, time of day, our own moods, and current preoccupations, there would always be something different to see. The anticipation was never knowing in advance what it would be: the enjoyment was discovering that it still had the capacity to surprise. Monumental figures in history are like that. They repay the repeated encounter and the probings of memory with endless new angles and unexpected revelations. So too monumental events, concepts, narratives.

At one meeting with Douglas in the early 1980s when I had been researching the maquis for a few years, I said that I had always been intrigued that de Gaulle had bestowed the prestigious Compagnon de la Libération honor on the communist maquis leader in the Limousin, Georges Guingouin. I then added that if Guingouin was potentially a regional monument in much the same way that de Gaulle had become a national one, did this suggest that de Gaulle was really more responsive to local resistance leaders than he was given credit for?

It seemed a good moment to rehearse the story that Lucie Aubrac had told me in 1979 for a broadcast on the BBC. It was her account of de Gaulle's visit to Marseille shortly after the Liberation when Raymond Aubrac was the regional Commissaire de la République. "Between the aperitif and the meal," she said, "I switched the place names on the main table, so that the General was no longer placed next to the Prefect and other notables but was sitting between local members of the maquis. He said not a single word throughout the whole meal."[2] Douglas agreed that de Gaulle was not exactly known for his sense of humor on such occasions, but on the issue of Georges Guingouin and regionalism we decided to return to the subject at a later date. I said I was about to interview Guingouin and would report back. Perhaps we could organize an occasion, we thought, to compare the national and the regional as parallel sites of French history or, still more, the specificity of place in the history of Resistance.

For all kinds of reasons we never got round to setting up such an occasion. Douglas continued to be warmly supportive of those of us working on regional and specific areas of Occupied France, and we, in turn, continued to be stimulated by his immense knowledge of French personalities and politics, and his singular understanding of de Gaulle and the French nation. My hoped-for meeting with Georges Guingouin failed to happen: he was unwell when I was due to visit him near Troyes in the Aube, and I got the impression that he no longer wanted to be interviewed, with good reason as it transpired. But the idea of weaving an argument about regionalism around a case study of Guingouin and the Limousin has never gone away. In this chapter, therefore, in tribute to Douglas as mentor, fellow historian, and friend, I would like to do what I had hoped to do then, leaving to our imagination what Douglas's angle of participation would have been.

Georges Guingouin died in October 2005, aged ninety-two. He invited a comparison with de Gaulle in the very first sentences of his account of his resistance activity, *Quatre ans de lutte sur le sol Limousin* (Four years of struggle on Limousin soil) published in 1974 in the series edited by Henri Michel on the Liberation of France. Although written in the third person, it was essentially a memoir. It began:

> 18 June 1940: from London, General de Gaulle addresses his compatriots. 18 June 1940, in Moulins-sur-Allier a wounded soldier deliberately leaves the military hospital of Sainte-Madeleine to avoid being taken prisoner by the Germans. He still has pinned to his blood-stained uniform the medical order from the front assigning him to a stretcher. . . . That wounded soldier was the village schoolmaster of Saint-Gilles-les-Forêts in the Haute-Vienne, Georges Guingouin.[3]

Within two weeks Guingouin was back at his village schoolhouse, teaching by day but sleeping in neighboring farms to avoid arrest. He was pursued by the police for demobilizing himself, and for continuing his role as a communist militant, secretary to the rural sector based on Eymoutiers.

So, June 18, 1940: two quite distinct gestures. Each at the origin of a long saga of resistance, and the making of a historic identity: de Gaulle as leader of Les Français libres and symbol of national resistance; Guingouin often called "the first maquisard" who dubbed himself in 1943–4 as "le préfet du maquis" ("Prefect of the Maquis"), and now features in the *Dictionnaire historique de la Résistance* as "the symbol of resistance in the Limousin" or in de Gaulle's own words, "the incarnation of civil resistance in the Limousin."[4]

Guingouin's call to the fight took two months to emerge but it finally did so in August 1940 in a long, closely argued, *Appel à la lutte* (Call to the fight), typed by Madame Lepage, a Parisian typist who had taken refuge close to Saint-Gilles-les-Forêts and was a "communist sympathiser."[5] Escalating from fifteen copies of this one-off "*Appel*" to a series of tracts meant reequipping the roneo of the local party sector. It was a typical way in which clandestine activity started: the creation of a web of communication, and the search for secure places for typing and duplicating to take place. Only in this case it was not in a town, where most resistance originated, but in the depths of the countryside, and the secure places were outlying farm buildings, and at one point inside a disused threshing machine, abandoned in the undergrowth of a wood.

It was Guingouin's rural remoteness, and his fertile sense of initiative which allowed him to develop his own communist voice in the period when the party at its center was deeply embroiled in the illusions and *mauvaise foi* of the Nazi–Soviet pact. The class-based communist rhetoric of his early tracts was orthodox enough, but he did not endorse the statements of neutrality which peppered the columns of the party's main paper, *L'Humanité*, throughout the autumn and winter of 1940–1.

By mid-1941 Vichy had put a price on his head and he had taken fully to clandestinity as "Raoul," eluding arrest by moving across the departmental border into the Corrèze and back again, living in barns and stone huts in the woods, frequently ill due to his war injury and his enforced style of life, and once close to dying, but protected and cared for by a number of remarkable peasant families, all the while creating his own network of resisters from inside and outside the party. Known in the local patois as "lou grand" (the tall one, not only de Gaulle), he was equally referred to as "the madman of the woods," while in Vichy police reports from late 1942 he constantly appears as "the dangerous communist, Guingouin, Georges, on the run . . . condemned to death in absentia."[6]

So here in shorthand notoriety we have the beginning and development of Guingouin's volatile, elusive, and effective maquisard career which led him to become a colonel in the Francs-Tireurs et Partisans Français (the FTP), and in mid-1944 commander in the Haute-Vienne of the combined resistance forces, the FFI, within the military region R5 radiating out from Limoges. But the reputation I want to address goes beyond his record as a maquis leader to one which suggests that he represented a region, the Limousin, even as de Gaulle came to represent France.

The Limousin as we know it is made up of the *départements* of the Haute-Vienne, the Creuse and the Corrèze. It is not one of the regions most normally evoked by historians when tracing the history of French regionalism since the eighteenth century. Its history seems unremarkable and none of its *beaux sites* carry sufficient Michelin stars to attract the tourist industry. On this side of the Channel I heard it once described as somewhere between the *châteaux* and the *foie gras*, between the Loire and the Périgord. At the time of the Roman invasion its people mostly belonged to the tribe of the Lémovices, and during the Carolingian empire, the *comté* of the Limousin, like the maquis fiefdom of Georges Guingouin centuries later, was said to have thrived on its isolation. The Limousin was part of Aquitaine until the tenth century, when its fluctuating borders and identity began to reflect its pivotal position between the Midi and the north of France. It was caught up in all the Anglo-French wars of the Middle Ages, and experienced long years of English occupation.

Limousin was a dialect of the Langue d'Oc and still more a literary language of the *troubadors*, almost identical to *provençal*. Move on to the eighteenth century and only then do urban elements begin to give the agricultural region a modern reputation: enamel and porcelain in Limoges, tapestry in Aubusson, and arms manufacturing in Tulle. Otherwise, it was a race of sturdy cattle on the central *plâteau des Millevaches* to which the name Limousin was most often attached. At some point in the early twentieth century, the word "limousine" was transferred from carriages to cars with a passenger section separate from the driver and protected from the elements, resembling, it was said, the protective bulk of the heavy overcoat, *la limousine*, worn by Limousin peasants. At much the same time, another quirk of etymology conveyed a sense of backwater status: in September 1914, 134 senior army officers judged incapable of running a campaign were sent by Joffre away from the war to barracks in Limoges, giving rise to the verb *limoger*, to dismiss or to expel.

These humiliated officers, forced to encounter the Limousin, were never to my knowledge transformed into regional heroes, but thirty years later in the expansion of resistance under the Occupation, there was a tendency to invert the meaning of "limoger" and bestow value on anyone dismissed, for whatever reason, by the new authority, Vichy.

It is tempting to delve more adequately into the background history of the region, but my aim in this chapter is to look at three mid-twentieth-century historical encounters with the Limousin, and conclude with a fourth, enigmatic encounter of my own in 2005.

I am using the concept of encounter in order to prioritize event and agency in the construction of a regional identity. Much, if not most, of regional consciousness is constantly reconstructed. How? When? and Why? provide the question marks.

Created? Constructed? Invented? Shaped? Imposed? They are all words which defy the hold that the word "essence" continues to exert over any discussion of either region or nation, particularly in the vocabulary of heritage. "Essence" and "essentialism" are rarely helpful words in historical explanation.

The use of active words and the primacy of events look like a repudiation of the structural concepts of the Annales school. But it isn't what it seems. The *longue durée* (long-term) structures, the geography, and the *mentalités* of the French regions have been meticulously and imaginatively researched by a host of scholars, and I find myself evoking them increasingly when situating behavior and events in the twentieth century. Similarly, I am keen to explore Pierre Bourdieu's structural concept of preconditioning, which he calls "habitus," but in doing so I would like to make it as historical and undeterministic as possible, without rejecting its key insights.

An event-driven, active approach was adopted by Jacques Revel when given the topic of "the region" by Pierre Nora for the third section of the pioneer volumes on collective memory, *Les lieux de mémoire*. He starts with a poster from the Gaullist youth organization in 1969, which proclaims "Yes to Youth. Yes to Region" and shows ebullient youths waving a *tricolor* flag and raising their arms in imitation of de Gaulle. Either Revel or the editors gave the illustration the caption "Does the region exist?" His answer is anchored in the reordering of the nation in the revolutionary period, and yes, he replies to his own question, the region does exist, as a product of this reordering.

In the eighteenth century, says Revel, there was no tight geographical, historical, or cultural definition of the region: it could be much smaller or much larger than the region which the twentieth century has formally come to accept, and this fluidity of definition and language is still there in the literature of today. The term "local" has become the shorthand for conveying this fluidity, and I acknowledge that I am probably guilty of overusing it, though it is now hugely present in the writings of French colleagues who work on similar topics. Revel's study of this fluid concept of the region begins with the statement that "The Revolution brutally modified the conditions of experience. . . . By asserting the absolute priority of national unity and providing the means for achieving it, the Revolution, in a sense, invented the regional issue, or rather brought it into the open and thereby made it unavoidable." In short, he argues, the breakup of the regions into *départements* does not obliterate the region, but, in fact, provokes a continuous encounter between each *département* and the region which enfolds it.[7]

It is precisely an active engagement with the region and the locality in the years of the Occupation that constitutes the first of the encounters I want to present.

Guingouin escaped from a military hospital in the Allier to return to his native Limousin at the same time as the mass civilian exodus of people escaping from the invading Germans. The *exode* forced an acute awareness of dislocation, relocation, and local distinctiveness. There had long been inchoate or closely knit groups of Limousin migrants in Paris who kept their regional origins alive, and who now attempted to return to their roots. Alongside their discourse of return there were the unfamiliar expressions of many refugees who arrived in the Limousin from other distinctive regions, notably Alsace and Lorraine. Regional origin and identity were the staple diet of observation, comment, exchange, and conflict. Personal memoirs and prefectoral reports vividly testify to this.

The division of France by the Armistice into separate zones, and the abolition of republican institutions by Vichy, furthered an awareness of the all-pervading reality of the region. It was enhanced by Vichy's establishment of regional prefects.Demand for food across regional boundaries was frequently met by protectionist measures within regions, while the resurfacing of archaic methods of production and subsistence merged with reanimated local folklore and superstition. There was a sense of confinement and constriction, but also of local resources, knowledge, and possibilities. They were all easily classified as regional.

Given this intense concentration on the local, Vichy's explicit provincial and regional agenda had everything in its favor. Yet it failed to realize its potential, losing its way in a plethora of elitist gestures and the vindictiveness of its anti-republicanism.

Despite this failure, regionalism as an idea or program remained associated after the war with the ideology of Vichy and the political Right. As a result the extent to which protest activity and resistance under the Occupation created its own form of regionalism was marginalized until well into the 1970s. Ex-resisters themselves often denied any regional causality in order to stress the national aim of liberation, and this downplayed the regional context as well as local motivation.

Yet no one can doubt that people in the Limousin (as elsewhere) encountered and interpreted the region under the Occupation in a multitude of tangible ways, even when it was the more limited concept of region, meaning *petit pays* or locality. In the Corrèze, the resisters of the Armée Secrète in the area of Neuvic, Egletons, and Ussel saw themselves as defined by the plateau and *pays* of the Haute-Corrèze rather than by the wider concept of the Limousin. Two of them who wrote the history of their resistance, Louis le Moigne and Marcel Barbanceys, show enormous self-awareness. There is one comment of theirs that I particularly savor: "In the region," they wrote, "people referred to the Germans as Chleuhs" (the name given to independent Berber tribes in the High Atlas mountains of Morocco). "In fact," the authors continue, "it was the maquis itself which truly played the role of Chleuhs vis-à-vis the regular German troops, unexpectedly firing at

German convoys before disappearing into the woods, only to re-emerge and start again further on."[8] From this one small sentence, let me, en passant, advocate that we read and borrow more from ethnological work on how and why the concept of tribalism is constructed. It is only very recently that it is beginning to be used to unlock patterns of belonging and behavior in groups under the Occupation.

Typologies of local resistance have certainly been created, and Guingouin had no doubt of the equivalence of the Limousin and resistance. Although he constantly stressed the national cause, he accentuated the regional range of his outlaw status as *préfet du maquis*; he equated his maquis territory with most of the Limousin, and he anchored his four years of *lutte sur le sol limousin* within the autonomous traditions of the Languedoc or Occitanie, elevating its provincial significance.

In terms of regional folklore Guingouin's legendary status in the countryside was thought by some to draw intentionally on the wellspring of popular religious custom in the Limousin, expressed in festival days, on which the supposed relics of local saints are displayed and paraded. Known as *ostensions,* these pious and festive displays of *sainte Martial, sainte Éloi, sainte Valérie,* and others, date back to the tenth century, but the belief systems they encode reach out to include the imagining of saints who continue to exist as hermits or miracle workers in the countryside. An early reputation gained by Guingouin, the "madman in the woods," when peasant families ran across him in hiding, or heard of his elusive existence, was less the label of "outlaw," "poacher," or "bandit" which soon came to clothe the image of maquisards, than the idea of a persecuted local visionary, ever close to death, who possessed intimate knowledge of local people and remarkable powers. Vichy's regional intelligence service, the *renseignements généraux,* unintentionally fed into this by their responsiveness to rumor, reporting Guingouin as seen in several different places at once and quoting repeated evidence of his mysterious re-appearance after certain death. By 1943–4, almost every audacious action in the Haute-Vienne and beyond was attributed to him, in person.

It would be absurdly fanciful to say that when he finally appeared at the Liberation, it was as a living relic, though the life and death knife-edge of his existence was evident twice just after the Liberation. First, he was fired at in Limoges by a would-be killer who was never discovered, and three weeks later the car he was driving veered off a country road he knew well and ploughed into trees, leaving him badly injured. The implication was that someone had tampered with the steering, and that the would-be assassins on either occasion could have been of any political persuasion, or none. The stories surrounding him tipped increasingly into mythology, a cue to comparison with Maurice Agulhon's *De Gaulle: histoire, symbole, mythe,* published by Plon in 2000, and much admired by Douglas.

Guingouin was also identified with regional promise. The marching song of his FTP in the Limousin pledged that the enemy would be defeated, Europe would change hands, and the belligerent proletariat would transform each province into a paradise, ending with the declamatory refrain "*Oui mais pour tous, oui pour tous, oui pour tous*" ("Yes but for all, yes for all, yes for all"). In his tracts he made it clear that his proletarians were the poor peasantry of the region, recalling the memory of the peasant rebels known as *croquants* under Henri IV, and it is agreed by all commentators that by the time of D-Day he was widely pictured in the rural Limousin as a tough, unifying, regional force. He nurtured the identity which active resistance gave to the Limousin, and which was acknowledged by de Gaulle after the Liberation when he nominated Limoges as the "Capital of the Maquis."

His uniqueness lay in understanding that, just as the region in Jacques Revel's words, "enfolded the *département*," so the maquisard territory of the Limousin hills and the forests enfolded Limoges. He rejected communist instructions to attack Limoges and provoke an urban insurrection, arguing that the rural depth of 20,000 FFI gave the resistance all the force it needed to negotiate a surrender by the heavily armed German garrison. An attack, he ruled, would result in needless civilian deaths in the inevitable German reprisals that would ensue. The surrender he worked toward was achieved on August 21, 1944, when a British and an American officer, who were individually in the region, were brought in to meet the German stipulation that they would sign only with Allied representatives.

At the very height of maquis activity, the region had been identified as a "little Russia" by de Vaugelas, commander of Vichy's Milice, who was sent across from the Rhône area into the Limousin with the order to root out the resistance in the region. This was also the instruction given by the German command to the Das Reich division of the SS which was moved up in June 1944 from the southwest specifically to take on the maquis and subdue the population, and only then to reinforce the German forces in the north.

The repression perpetrated by the SS had its appalling climax in the hangings of 99 men at Tulle in the south of the region, and the massacre of 643 men, women, and children at Oradour-sur-Glane, close to Saint Junien to the west of Limoges. These inhuman atrocities clearly affected Guingouin's decision not to risk a bloodbath in Limoges. But there were not even theoretical plans in his mind for the capture of the urban garrison. His maquis had fought its ground against German troops at Mont Gargan, close to his village of Saint-Gilles-les-Forêts, and had not evaporated. His priority had always been to make resistance effective in his rural locality. This he had achieved.

In August 1944 de Gaulle took national power by acclamation. Guingouin, the regional symbol, still a communist, was elected mayor of Limoges in 1945.

The extent to which the Limousin had gained a self-consciously regional identity under the Occupation was starkly revealed, intensified, and changed by events almost eight years later in 1953, the second of the historical encounters.

Clearly moved by the atrocity of Oradour-sur-Glane, General de Gaulle declared in 1945 that the ruins should be preserved in perpetuity as a national memorial site. Bringing those responsible for the massacre to trial was a regional priority. It was the third company of the regiment Der Führer belonging to the SS Panzer division Das Reich, who had perpetrated the atrocities in the Limousin. The commander of the SS Das Reich was General Heinz Lammerding. In Bordeaux in 1951 he was condemned to death in absentia for the hangings at Tulle. Although his whereabouts in Germany were known, the British authorities in that zone refused to send him to France for the trial. Anger was widely expressed in the region. The families of the victims of Oradour-sur-Glane nevertheless expected that he would be extradited for the Oradour trial, scheduled once again to take place in Bordeaux. The British maintained their refusal. Lammerding was too useful, it was later surmised, to the Cold War intelligence of the West.

When the trial finally opened in January 1953, twenty-one soldiers had been found to stand trial. Seven were Germans who had been kept in French prisoner-of-war camps, and to the surprise of international commentators though not to French journalists, fourteen were French. They came from Alsace. One was a volunteer for the German army, the thirteen others had been conscripted in the annexed region by force, some underage at the time. All were part of the Der Führer company which descended on Oradour. The Nuremburg tribunal had confirmed that German conscription by force in Alsace, and occupied territories elsewhere, was itself a war crime. The thirteen from Alsace, therefore, stood as symbols of the two hundred thousand men, the *malgré nous* (constrained by force) mobilized by the Germans. Accused in Bordeaux as perpetrators, the thirteen were defended within Alsace as victims of Nazi occupation.

The story of this sensational trial has been clearly told by the American historian Sarah Farmer in her remarkable study of Oradour, titled *Martyred Village*, while the case for the *malgré nous* as presented in Alsace during the trial has been analyzed with scholarly passion by Jean-Laurent Vonau in 2003. All the ingredients are there of the bitter, emotional clash between the two regions, Limousin and Alsace, for that is exactly what the trial became. The content, both legal and political, was intricate, difficult, and ambiguous. But the regional investment from both the Limousin and Alsace was stark and polarizing.

To turn from the Limoges-based socialist paper, *Le Populaire du Centre* with its cries for justice against all who had perpetrated the massacre, regardless of how they came to be there, to turn from this to the *malgré nous* commitment of *Le Nouveau Rhin français* is to find a Strasbourg restaurateur, once a local commander, like Guingouin, of the FFI, tearing up his Légion d'Honneur in front of his restaurant. This made front page cover of the repeated protests against the trial all over Alsace, and the symbolic shrouding of the Strasbourg war memorial in black. On the platforms of the Strasbourg railway station people coming and going were heard greeting each other with the defiantly ironic, "Salut, assassin."[9]

The reaction across the Limousin to this unexpectedly visceral rejection of the Bordeaux trial was initially one of incomprehension: it was imagined that a national consensus had been reached in 1945 on the iconic status of Oradour and that French public opinion would respect a law passed in 1948 making all members of any military unit that committed a war crime collectively responsible, even when the law was revoked during the trial.

Opinion in Alsace stressed the sufferings and torture endured by the *malgré nous*, and the incidence of their deaths on the Eastern Front which exceeded other statistics of French military loss during the war. Once the trial proceeded, and the judges brought sentences of guilt against the accused, the outcry in Alsace was deemed to be so threatening to French unity that an amnesty covering those conscripted by force was hurriedly introduced by the government. The thirteen Alsace prisoners were allowed to go free. They returned to an emotional welcome in their localities. The lone Alsace volunteer and one of the German soldiers received death sentences, but these were commuted. All those imprisoned were released by 1958.

The French government, parliament, and public had been pulled in both directions, but this political cutting of the Gordian knot was bitterly resented in the Limousin. It was interpreted as a flagrant disregard for a poor, dominantly peasant, left-wing region in the face of a heavily populated and industrialized Alsace, the touchstone of patriotic French commitment since 1870.

Throughout the Bordeaux trial the familiar dialectic of center and margin, of Paris and province, was paralleled by encounters of region with region, and the two regions with themselves.

At the Liberation, the Limousin had been imaged as the center of the maquis with its epic narrative, on the one hand, and rampant German and Milice atrocities, on the other. There was pride in the Limousin that the conflict had made the region a vivid microcosm of what might be called the glory and the sorrow of 1944. Now, in 1953, opinion in the region angrily saw itself as abandoned by the nation and the victim of political discrimination. The Association of the Families of the Martyrs of Oradour sent back the Croix de Guerre and the Croix de la Légion d'honneur awarded to Oradour, refused to entertain government officials at the annual commemoration, and posted the names of politicians who had voted for the amnesty at the entry to the ruins.

The simple *Souviens-toi* (Remember) on the path leading to the site now had a double meaning.

Shortly after the trial came the climax of the third historical encounter, which is still full of mystery and skulduggery.

On December 24, 1953, Georges Guingouin was suddenly arrested, accused of complicity in a double murder perpetrated in the Limousin countryside shortly after the war. He was imprisoned at Brive, in the south of the region. Two months later, on February 23, 1954, the national news announced that he had made a suicide attempt in his cell, a sure sign, declared his accusers, of his guilt.

The chicanery, deceit, and conspiracy involved to get him arrested went back to 1944 at least. The imbroglio featured the Stalinist mania of the Communist Party at the time; the revenge of ex-Vichy police officers; the jealousy of several socialist notables of Limoges; and the venality of a few individuals in the country areas which had been controlled by Guingouin's maquis. The cacophony of accusations against Guingouin was orchestrated publicly in 1945 by the determined anti-communism of Jean-Louis Vigier, the eminent right-wing resistance editor of a postwar national paper, *L'Époque*. Vigier's own courage in German hands had involved an attempt to escape from repeated bouts of torture by jumping out of a prison window in Pont-Saint-Esprit in the Gard, injuring himself permanently. He survived the imminence of execution, and after the war became mayor of Pont-Saint-Esprit. He could not accept that the communist Guingouin, whom he described as a deserter and a bandit, should be mayor of Limoges. In repeated articles he accused him of having terrorized the countryside, and he denounced him for pillage and corruption.

The articles in *L'Époque* challenged the legendary status of the *préfet du maquis* at the most vulnerable point of any local resistance record: the climate of rumor, accusation, and the settling of scores, which affected the Liberation. The question of how far lives were distorted by this climate of suspicion, and how many innocent people were picked on by groups representing the resistance, has been impressively researched in the last twenty-five years. There has been a return to considering what Vigier called *l'envers du maquis*, the dark side of the armed struggle, while at the same time there have been correctives to the more exaggerated estimates of those killed in the *épuration* (the purge), which varied hugely across localities.

Guingouin succeeded in showing that *L'Époque* had no evidence to back its accusations against him, and Vigier was fined for his intemperate articles.

But Guingouin was also under sustained attack in 1945 from the other side of the political spectrum, from the leadership of the Communist Party, which demoted him at the local party level, and demanded a recantation of his independent attitudes during the war. This he refused, relying on his regional reputation to speak for itself, but standing increasingly on his own, without a reliable political base. In 1947 he lost the local elections to the Socialists, and returned to school teaching.

With Cold War rhetoric, the communist press raised the level of denunciation. In Stalinist language he was an "enemy of the worst kind," a regional Tito or a demented Trotskyist. He defended himself rigorously, expressing his self-belief that he was a true communist, but his independent record was the crucial issue. He was expelled from the party in December 1952. The pathological Stalinist purge of wartime leaders by communist parties across Europe reached into the rural fastness of the Limousin.

Even before his expulsion, the number of radically different attacks on Guingouin thickened the various plots against him. In unholy alliance, the Communist Party and the anti-communist *L'Époque* seized on rumors, or half-truths, of maquis vendettas, robberies, and killings and attached them to the *préfet du maquis*, substantiating a case already being formed against him by two shadowy ex-Vichy police inspectors, known only at the time by their initials "C" and "A," who used what later emerged as false testimonies, to indict him for complicity in murder.

The voices raised against him at the local level severely tarnished his image as a regional talisman. It was widely accepted that there had been summary executions in Limoges at the Liberation, whether or not he was ultimately responsible. He decided he would have to move out of the region. His wife Henriette had come from the Aube and it was in that *département* that they accepted a joint school post at the *rentrée* (return to school) of 1952. It was from the Aube that he went in good faith to give evidence at his trial in Brive, but was arrested and thrown into prison.

The news of the suicide attempt gave way to reports that he had suffered a total loss of reason, smashing his cell and threatening to kill the warders with a piece of glass. Henriette had refused to accept the news as fact and had raced to Brive. Despite her intervention, a desperately ill Guingouin was transferred to Toulouse prison, but denied adequate medical attention, until renewed pressure from Henriette succeeded in getting him moved, in a coma, to the local psychiatric hospital. There he gradually began to recover. All evidence of what had actually happened at Brive was suppressed by those who were in a position to know. It later transpired that he was probably attacked by two men, beaten up, and left for dead, but the eyewitness evidence for this, and the possibility of tracking down his assailants, eluded an official investigator, whose report nevertheless severely questioned the conduct of the prison authorities. The TV journalist, Michel Taubmann, quoted extracts from a draft of this report in his reconstruction of the whole intricate sequence of events, which he published in 1994 as *L'Affaire Guingouin* after seven years of research.

Henriette Guingouin did not act alone. She had the support of the Association of ex-resisters in the Toulouse *département* of the Haute-Garonne, which issued a coruscating series of questions, likened by some to Zola's *J'accuse* at the time of the Dreyfus affair. It convinced the national Ligue des Droits de l'Homme (League of Human Rights) to take up Guingouin's cause, which he himself began to fight, once he was granted provisional freedom back in the Aube, all the while still technically awaiting trial.

On May 20, 1969, Douglas Johnson gave his inaugural lecture at University College, London, in which he focused on three episodes in French history, all meeting in the year 1954. He said, "I want to talk about the French war in Indo-China, the European Defence Community Treaty, and the war in Algeria. All three of these have been separately called, by different historians, 'the Dreyfus Affair of the Fourth Republic.'"[10] The reference was to the divisive nature of all three episodes: friend pitted against friend, families disagreeing over the *midi* meal, tables overturned. I have deliberately continued his choice of year and theme. In the same year, 1954, at the regional level, the Guingouin affair prompted several references back to the Dreyfus affair in terms of its divisiveness but equally because of its injustice. It is easy to see why.

In the Limousin itself, the leading Socialists and Communists, disputing power in the Limoges area, vied with each other to find evidence of misdeeds in Guingouin's resistance past, and allowed fabricated stories to circulate, not just in the region but nationwide. In this context the friends of Guingouin, who created a Defence Committee in Limoges, found themselves having to uncover testimony of Guingouin's integrity which had previously been taken for granted: the Protestant pastor, Albert Chaudier, was President of the Haute-Vienne's Liberation Committee and had evaluated Guingouin honorably as above suspicion, *un pur.* The collective memory of the region was at stake.

It took five years for Guingouin to clear his name. In 1959 it was finally judged that he had no case to answer. The web of falsehoods in the various charges of murder or complicity was fully exposed, but his treatment in prison remained obscured by officialdom and conflicting memory.

In many ways Guingouin's principal support, and the ultimate strength of the local defense committee, came from outside the region, from the solidarity shown by a good number of national resistance figures. On the noncommunist-left the moral force of Claude Bourdet was particularly effective: he was penetrating in his 1955 article in *France-Observateur* in which he asked accusingly, "Who drove Guingouin mad?" Others who spoke or wrote publicly in his defense included the eminent authors François Mauriac and Jean-Marie Domenach, and General de Gaulle himself. Guingouin's committed advocate was the young Parisian lawyer Roland Dumas.

Was it significant that Dumas came originally from Limoges? Perhaps. But he could only be adduced as one voice on one side of the Guingouin affair.

There was no regional consensus. Nor was there a great deal of interest outside France, partly I suspect due to reaction to the Drummond Affair. In the summer of 1952, the British scientist Sir Jack Drummond, a onetime professor of biochemistry at University College, London, his wife Anne, and their ten-year-old daughter Elizabeth were brutally murdered while on holiday near the village of Lurs in the Durance valley in Provence. The 77-year-old peasant farmer, Gaston Dominici, who spoke only patois, was found guilty in November 1954. His death sentence was commuted in 1957 and he was released on compassionate grounds by President de Gaulle in 1960.

Just to mention the tragic Drummond case can still trigger a certain phobia about French rural society, but also a fascination with rumored spy and resistance dimensions to the story, and a conviction that it was one of the many unsolved crimes of the Cold War. There has been an undiminished obsession with Gaston Dominici as either an innocent or a ruthless peasant patriarch, and certainly a man from the past.

Throughout 1954 when Guingouin was in prison in Brive and Toulouse, Gaston Dominici alternately confessed and withdrew his confession. His family deepened the mystery with their conflicting testimonies and intergenerational feuding.

The image of a backward and atavistic peasant mentality threatened to dominate the French press, disputing space with the escalation of Poujadisme among small-town shopkeepers and the peasantry of certain areas. To say the very least, it was not a time when it was easy for anyone to do justice to the history of rural resistance.

Guingouin's reputation was battered and scarred by the accusations against him. He needed the press to take the testimony of his fellow Limousin maquisards seriously. But how many journalists or historians were interested in doing so? Any evidence from individual peasant farmers, traders, or workers became generally suspect, resistance memories especially so, particularly if they came from communists. The testimonies of regional and rural resisters were considered inevitably flawed. To the Cold War of the 1950s must be added an urban–rural divide.

Yes, Guingouin was crucially backed by national resisters and benefited from their advocacy in certain influential media. But the bulk of the press encouraged readers to see the whole affair as yet more evidence of impenetrable rural backwaters. The journalist Pascal Parisot, writing in the international review *Preuves* at the height of the Guingouin affair was unerringly accurate. "This is the trial of peasant resistance in one of the poorest regions of France which figures on the economic map solely as a source of chestnuts."[11]

From all the defamation of the 1950s, Guingouin fought back to become once again a significant symbol of the Limousin. The key was not only the historical significance of his Resistance, however controversial, but also his independence. Like de Gaulle he developed, through his Resistance, a distinctive political persona, which defied party-political norms. In 1998 Robert Hue apologized to him on behalf of the Communist Party for its mistakes and maltreatment, a major reappraisal of party history. In 1999 the authorities of France, Alsace, and the Limousin finally joined together at Oradour to launch the new Centre de la Mémoire, and in 2005 Guingouin was promoted to Commandeur of the Légion d'Honneur.

There has been only one certain way in which Guingouin has been fully rehabilitated: through a long process of regional rediscovery and the construction of a new form of regionalism which creates its own modern identity, escaping from nostalgia, and from the crippling view that the idea of "the region" was a shibboleth of reactionary ideology. Today, this new construction has happened, and it is happening still. Regional articulation of modern identity is in crescendo mode and emerges in surprising and unpredictable ways, which brings me to my fourth, and personal, encounter.

June 5, 2005, was a sunny Sunday morning. I was just south of Limoges en route to a rendezvous at Saint-Gilles-les-Forêts with one of Guingouin's original neighbors, and a commemoration to the memory of Violette Szabo, the SOE agent who was dropped into a nearby village on June 7, 1944. On a small byroad I stopped at the old medieval château de Châlucet. There was nobody about; the birds were singing loudly, a cuckoo echoing through the dense woods which enfold the towering ruins. The information at the base of the site gave details of its occupation by the English during the Hundred Years' War. I walked up to the top to enjoy the dominance of the château over the river Briance. I saw no one. An hour later I returned to my small right-hand drive car in the shade of the trees at the bottom, to find a chalk message written across the door, "Toujours l'ennemi" (Still the Enemy).

Why "toujours"? Who, and where, was the person who needed to make the connection between medieval hostilities and 2005? I never discovered. I thought it might be a reference to the visible occupation of parts of the countryside by English property buyers. Other evidence suggested a more current political motive.

The week before, on May 29, France had voted solidly Non against the new European Constitution. In the Limousin, just under 60 per cent of the votes were Non. President Chirac had told the French nation that the EU had no secondary plan if the Constitution was rejected: there was no plan B. Oh yes there was, many people were saying: it was at the very heart of the newly proposed Constitution, the B of Blair and Britain, the kind of Europe which they saw as the imposition on the EU of an Anglo-American neoliberal economy. At Châlucet, anonymously chalked on my car, it is probable that the region's archaic memory of the English Occupation and this particular passion over the future of Europe were succinctly brought together.

I asked myself if this gesture would be recognized by Pierre Nora as the continuing impact of a *lieu de mémoire*? I needed to ask that question, because my visit to the Limousin was basically to continue researching the memory of local contestation and protest across the twentieth century. I was there to attend the centenary of the 1905 revolt of porcelain workers in Limoges and it was precisely in acts of public commemoration that Nora had situated the survival and articulation of collective memory in contemporary France.

The relationship between regional memory and the "red Spring of Limoges in 1905," *le printemps rouge de Limoges*, was brilliantly explored in a superb exhibition at the Archives départementales, and developed with sophisticated historical theory in the accompanying text. The authors showed that for much of the century the dramatic events of 1905 were central to the construction of individual and collective identities in the region.[12]

The historical process was extended to the whole of the Limousin in a series of public lectures, published in book form in 2005 and creating an image of the twentieth century locally as a militant century, *Un Siècle militant*. Scholarly research showed that the Limousin was the recurrent site of militant protest. The book could legitimately have begun at the start of the century, taking the revolt of 1905 against appalling conditions of work as its key, but, instead, it placed at the beginning two long research articles on the maquis activities in the region, as if to state that the collective identity of the Limousin in the twentieth century was most firmly expressed and rooted in the response to the Occupation. To borrow from de Gaulle once again, one could say that the Limousin had "married its century."

These first two research articles reaffirmed Georges Guingouin's sound judgment in not attacking Limoges, and showed the precocity of the Limousin maquis in their close understanding, both political and economic, of the attitudes and needs of the local peasantry.[13]

The book then ranged backward and forward. It highlighted the independent mentality of the region in its worker–peasant dissidence and commitment to action. It did not avoid conflicting evidence. There is no regional complacency. But in total, several decades of historical enquiry into the region culminated in this assessment of a militant political identity, at the forefront of which was the Limousin maquis, with its totemic mix of rural activism and visionary leadership.

The Guingouin defence committee of the 1950s had long ago begun the re-valorization of the *préfet du maquis*. The work of the committee had its own forensic imperative. Its ultimate inheritors were the associations and pressure groups which mushroomed in the last twenty years of the twentieth century to produce numerous collective statements of the region's political and social mentality. Sites of action have been marked on hills, in villages, and towns;

plaques and monuments erected; biographies researched; museums and exhibitions opened.

Guingouin himself was the founder-president of the association pressing for a resistance museum for the Haute-Vienne. Its activities have been of critical historical value. It has provided vital details of the new social categories created during the resistance, giving particular prominence to the long-neglected roles of women such as Maria Boudarias, one of the most active *mères du maquis*, whose family farm at Mouret was the first of Guingouin's early hiding places, and whose initiative and *savoir-faire* became legendary in the clandestine movements of the region.[14]

I believe it to be demonstrable that the reassessment of memory and identity at the end of the twentieth century, and the start of this one, has affected France most intriguingly at the regional level. Perhaps one could argue that the decline of a unifying national narrative in France has given space for the rise of regional ones, and that Jean-Marie Guillon's phrase can be reapplied as *le local domine le national* (the local dominates the national). Research and enterprise within many French regions are resulting in the documentation of a specific twentieth-century identity, which the heritage movement is beginning to take seriously. The idea of patrimony does not have to be located solely or even primarily in the very *longue durée*, whatever a chalked message at Châlucet might imply. Structures and predispositions continue to be created. They were constructed in abundance in the twentieth century. Potent memories too; and memories are not just about recall and remembering: they are active agents in the construction of new identities.

Douglas Johnson, perceptive and realistic, knew that in writing or lecturing on any aspect of France there is always a counter-lecture that could be given. We both knew that another angle could be found. Whatever the subject, we enjoyed discussing alternatives. With reference, as ever, to General de Gaulle, does this amount to agreeing that everyone has his/her own *certaine idée de la France*? Yes, indeed, but not if it means a reductionism to where everything is seen as equally valid. There is always the need to evaluate. In this chapter I have chosen to give a version of regional encounters. I know that in the region itself it might well be disputed. But in all controversy there is a necessity to choose. At an everyday level this necessity is captured in a colorful Midi postcard showing the telling challenge of one café to another, boldly written over the outside door: *Mieux vaut boire ici qu'en face* (Better to drink here than opposite). We invariably come back to that. Specificity is also choice.

*   *   *

In 1980, Lucien Maury, a schoolteacher south of Carcassonne in the département of the Aude, between the Pyrenees and the Mediterranean, had edited and presented two volumes on local resistance, titled simply La Résistance audoise. *On the back cover of each volume a long blurb started by saying that the subject of the Resistance had for years stirred passions both negative and positive. "Here," it claimed, "the Resisters of the Aude speak for themselves." ("Ici les Résistants audois vous parlent.") On June 24, 1982, I went to meet Lucien Maury and his wife Françoise at their home in Quillan.*

M. Lucien MAURY

A large proportion of the Aude is covered with forests, but a maquis needed water as well. Picaussel [to the west of Quillan] was almost a model maquis area, and excellent for parachute drops, being well above the local German headquarters. The population was favorable for three reasons. The leaders were known to them: both I and my adjoint were local schoolteachers. Our contacts with London carried status. And, third, the ancient Cathar mentality was still alive, an old tradition of liberty and resistance just as strong as in the struggles against Simon de Montfort in the early thirteenth century. There was a kind of Languedoc inheritance which was important. Catharism for some conjures up a country of troubadors, courtly love, and an easy life in the sun. But it was a tough and difficult religion resisting the abuses of Catholicism. I have no doubt that Catharism was still the spirit of Resistance. But the struggle against the Germans was different from the struggles of the Cathars against the north of France. Resistance was based on the unity of the French. The origins of the maquis cannot therefore be sought in the regionalism of the Cathars. I come from the Ariège [adjacent to the Aude], but I have never felt any less French than the Parisians.

Both my wife and I spoke Occitan from time to time. It was useful for making good relations with the peasantry. Schoolteachers were very close to the population. . . . I must also point out my temperament as a keen rugby player. We had a combative nature. There were many rugby players in the maquis.

When peasants were on our side we arrived for provisions as if they were hostile. A little bit of theater was staged to make it look as if they had no choice. But where peasants were really against us, then we cut out the playacting, making our raids at night. On the whole these were a rarity, but they were barbaric really, the darkest point of the Resistance. They were grave mistakes. It allowed all abuse to be imputed to the Resistance. Of course, there was abuse. But the vast majority of the crimes of the period were not committed by the maquis. We were not bandits.

Mme. Françoise MAURY

I was also a schoolteacher. When my husband was hunted by the Gestapo, he left his job as a teacher and signed up in the Beaux Arts in Toulouse as cover. While he was away there was a parachute drop. I made up a code on the spur of the moment and sent him the message. The role of women was equal to that of men. Everywhere there was an absence of men, due to the number of prisoners of war. In the film, *Lacombe Lucien*, far too much importance was given to accident, not enough to choice. And I found *Le Chagrin et la Pitié* unsatisfactory: it concentrated too much on the unusual aspects. The schoolmaster in *Lacombe Lucien* refused to accept Lucien into the maquis. We never refused anyone, though we studied them carefully: some of the very young ones could have been set up by the Vichy Milice.[15]

6

The Némirovsky Effect

It appears that the playful philosopher, Jean Baudrillard, died in March 2007. "It appears" would have been his own choice of language, with his preference for the concept of simulation over any other, more concrete, way of rendering fact and event. His love of paradox and upside-down thinking was infectious and often very funny: "Nobody needs French theory" was his favorite line in self-denial.

In two areas his creative talents were outstanding: he was an inspired photographer of things, while at the heart of his philosophy lay the idea that simulation, simulacra, make-believe, the "as if," had become the new reality. He was credited with predicting the hold of virtual reality in today's culture; and being just ahead of the technology gave him the instant role of prophet, wit, scourge, and stoic of the new era. His status was evident by the late 1980s. Even as many of us celebrated the Bicentenary of the French Revolution in 1989 in the Place de la Bastille wearing ill-fitting Phrygian bonnets, François Furet had made us skeptical of the received narrative of revolution, but Baudrillard made "simulation" into a word with genuinely revolutionary connotations. It took us into an elusive, exciting, inchoate world which lay beyond the distinctions between the fictional and the real.

The art critic Adrian Searle saw the photographs of Baudrillard as "wistful, elegaic and oddly haunting . . . like movie stills of unregarded moments."[1] The Némirovsky effect, no less than these photographs, has challenged us to take very seriously the realm of the "unregarded."

In approaching Némirovsky we need to be aware of the ever-expanding parameters of the reality debate, a pursuit of reality which has television entertainment, the internet, and journalism of all kinds snapping at the heels of historians, with a zeal and marketing capacity as sharp as the culinary industry in pursuit of "real food." History, it emerges from many quarters of the media, is real only when it is revealed as having been hidden, occluded, deliberately obscured, forgotten, skewed, traduced. It is not just a vested interest in sensation. We have all been part of making history synonymous with discovery: it is our professional mission statement. Yet, in the new drive to discover, there is a kind of revelatory zest which appeals, as Dan Brown exemplifies, not just to resurgent mystics, lovers of the occult, and enthusiasts of codes and dissimulation, but to a new mass audience, ready to take on the historical establishment.

The role of fiction and invention in purveying reality and controlling opinion has probably never been so prominent. Christian Salmon's exposé of today's fictional boom follows on from Baudrillard's perceptions. Co-founder of the International Parliament of Writers in 1993, Salmon writes powerfully on the public relations industry in the United States and the universal legacy of Edward Bernays, nephew of Freud, and the way in which the PR industry has increasingly ransacked Roland Barthes and Guy Debord to give intellectual credibility to its practices. The title gives it all away: *"Storytelling: La machine à fabriquer des histoires, et à formater les esprits"* ("Storytelling: The Machine for Fabricating Stories and Formatting Minds").[2] Only marginally are historians implicated in the production of the story line fictions which have replaced statistics and graphs in selling products or in justifying foreign policy; but having the same word for history and story has given the French a wider reaction to the whole world of "storytelling management." I have always liked the cartoon of the mid-1930s of Alfred Dreyfus, with his little son on his knee who is ready for bed and is calling out, *"Père, père, une histoire"* ("Daddy, Daddy, Tell me a story"). Dreyfus looks wearily resigned.

I was doing research at Tours in the Loire valley when the news broke. It was spring 2004 and a young French colleague told me over a glass of Chinon rouge that a recovered book from the time of the Occupation was causing huge excitement in Paris.

Written by Irène Némirovsky, it was said to be outrageously critical, or acutely realistic, toward ordinary French people in the first two years of the war. She was a successful Russian Jewish author, an *émigrée* in France from the Bolshevik Revolution and passionately anti-communist, who had been secretly writing her book in Issy l'Évêque on the edge of the Morvan hills of northern Burgundy in the Occupied zone. She talked of the imminence of deportation, but expected protection by people with influence in anti-Semitic right-wing circles in Paris. She did not try to escape to parts of France in the south which she knew well. On July 13, 1942, she was taken, as a foreign Jew, to a nearby detention center by the French police. She was deported on July 16 by the Germans to Auschwitz where she died of typhus a month later. She was thirty-nine.

Her precious manuscript in tiny, cramped handwriting had survived in the hands of one of her young daughters, Denise, who had been hidden for the remainder of the Occupation. For four decades its existence remained unknown.

The extraordinary history and amazing survival of the book was the first sensation.

Its content was the second.

Within months it was being hailed as the real story of the mass flight (*exode*) from the Germans in May–June 1940, and a revelation of the reality of the Occupation. Its title, *Suite française,* carried a musical charge: a series of movements, each one individual in its notation and its dynamics—an unfinished symphony of sharp tonal contrasts and achingly beautiful harmony.[3]

"Storm in June," the tempestuous allegro which opens the novel, is not the political tumult of defeat. It is a storm of French behavior and emotions at the heart of the *exode*. Caustic, parodic, wickedly perceptive, and yet also tender, romantic, rhapsodic even, its characters are an array of egotistical, conniving, proud, self-righteous, but also naive and well-meaning, recognizable simulacra of ordinary French people. There is the dissonance of class, the dialectic of mass and elite: it contains a strident fortissimo of hypocrisy. Pétain is absent in person and impact, but the ruralist idyll of Pétainism and Vichy, the romance of the countryside and the land, is very much there, and it pervades the whole of Part Two, the quiet after the storm.

If there is a resolution suggested by Némirovsky to "Storm in June," it lies in this second movement, marked as "Dolce," in the barely ruffled calm of an occupied rural community, complete with spring sounds, colors, and birdsong, and with arpeggios from the musical fingers of the billeted German officer, Lieutenant Bruno von Falk, or, rather, what she describes as a "palpitation of notes," symbol of the stirrings of sexual desire, human courtship, and male jealousy between occupied and occupiers.

In all respects, the publication grabbed the headlines. The alluring sepia photograph on the cover showed the intelligent young author in an elegant fur, fixing the reader with a penetrating, sad, and yet knowing gaze.

She had died as a victim of the Holocaust. That fact alone gave her an indisputable moral and historical force.

What was seen as its honest confrontation of realities, and its eyewitness veracity, gave it documentary power. It was praised for its dramatic and evocative prose, the quality of its insights into flawed or vulnerable behavior, and the beauty of its rural descriptions. Its sympathetic portrayal of the German occupiers made it a book for the twenty-first century: a break with taboos, a rejection of old antagonisms.

Here, apparently, was the France of the defeat and the early Occupation laid bare.

At the end there were other jottings, conveying the possible outlines of three further parts. She appears skeptical of history. She was at pains to stress the imaginative and inventive role of the novelist. "Never forget," she wrote to herself on June 2, 1942, that the war will be over and that the whole historical side will fade away. Try to create as much as possible: things, debates . . . that will interest people in 1952 or 2052. Re-read Tolstoy. Inimitable descriptions, but not historical. Insist on that. . . . Historical events are only a backdrop to a deep exploration of the human heart: one can skim over historical facts, but penetrate deeply into daily life, its affective side . . . and above all the comedy it presents.[4]

She uses the word "comedy" as in Balzac's *Comédie humaine,* doing what fiction does so well, exploring affective, emotional, interpersonal relationships, and effectively breaking the boundaries between private and public.

The Némirovsky event in 2004 had just this effect. "Skimming over historical fact" was not the message that was received, but "penetrating deeply into daily life, its affective side" chimed perfectly with the pursuit of reality. The most fascinating angle is that this explicit pursuit was once the trademark of modernist narratives seeking to move the sense of the past and present away from exclusive high politics toward social and cultural inclusion. By 2004 it was increasingly an area of post-modern research, journalism, and performance which occupied a no-holds-barred, confident, investigative terrain, frequently illuminating, but equally mythmaking in its play with relativism and its enthusiasm to demythologize the narratives which claimed to be liberating. We are still caught up in the crosscurrents, paradoxes, and conflicting aims of this reality debate.

Némirovsky had been writing a biography of Chekhov at the same time as *Suite française*. Particularly outside France, in the United States and the United Kingdom, the very "truthfulness" of Chekhov was ascribed to *Suite française*. The self-seeking debasement which is central to her portraits of the *exode* was seized on as the reality of French behavior in 1940, or the reality of French behavior at any time, finally rescued from the contrived oblivion of national memory. Still more, the "Dolce" of the relationships between French and Germans was praised as the reality of the early Occupation, finally unearthed from what were seen as the impacted layers of Resistance and Gaullist mythologies. Reviewers of other books on the Occupation found themselves referring to *Suite française* as if it were a factual record: the "as if," the simulation, taken for the immediacy of historical reality. Of course, it was acknowledged as representation, but what a pedigree it had. As the details of her life and other works emerged, thanks largely to the perceptive first biography by American Jonathan Weiss, her close relationships with *Gringoire*, and other publications and personalities of the extreme right, were interpreted as vital evidence of a certain Jewish reality held to be occluded by Holocaust history. The question of what was real, and what had been covered over, in the history of Jews in modern France took on an extra dimension.

Her savage portrait of a Jewish financier, his wife, and his daughter, in her novel of 1929, *David Golder*, appeared to give legitimacy to the anti-Semitic stereotypes of the interwar years, an accusation put into context by her subsequent biographers, Olivier Philipponnat and Patrick Lienhardt.[5]

I have heard "Storm in June" described at various times in the media as the ultimate unmasking of France, and "Dolce" as the first true picture of Franco–German relationships, an intimate reality hidden from the French, by the French, for over sixty years. Self-appointed Anglo-Saxon moralizers who take any opportunity to teach the French how to face up to their past have used the novel to expose French complacency. Apostles of postmodernism, who necessarily can't be seen to agree on anything, nevertheless combine to use the book to deconstruct any national myth that is thought to be peculiarly French, and certainly the heroic story of *le peuple* as defended by Régis Debray.

To take a step back and give ourselves a way of approaching the whole debate, we could flout the intention of Némirovsky and see *Suite française* as a variant of the historical novel. I looked at Susan Sontag's prescriptive essay on how to be a novelist in the media age, written just before her death in the same year as *Suite française* was published. I found one very relevant gem of advice: "Take care to be born at a time when . . . you would be definitely influenced by Dostoevsky, and Tolstoy, and Turgenev, and Chekhov . . ." and she continued to say that a great writer both creates and responds: that is, "responds to the world the writer shares with other people, but is unknown or mis-known by still more people . . . call that history, society, what you will."[6]

Beyond doubt, Sontag would have distinguished Némirovsky the writer from "the Némirovsky effect" and that would certainly be my view. But at the same time it is far from my intention to minimize or parody the effect. On the contrary, *Suite française*, has become one of the most-read books on the Occupation, particularly outside France. It has reached audiences that historians can only dream about. Its activating appeal has been nothing short of astounding. It has already attracted thousands to the quiet and still remote agricultural village of Issy l'Evêque, looking for ways of identifying the houses and places of the novel. I find this a hugely encouraging sign that people want to make the places of history real for themselves. In 2007, the year I visited the village, you could find a simple silver plaque on the house at the bottom of the village square where the novel was written, and a set of street names, suggesting several textual readings. On the plaque she is remembered as *Femme de lettres* and not as either Jewish or an immigrant, but the narrative of Vichy as permanently unacceptable is reinforced by the statement that she and her husband Michel Epstein were arrested, not by the French police but by "the Vichy police." Similarly, opposite the Hôtel des Voyageurs where she first lived and wrote at the start of the Occupation, there is a place where roads meet, not really a square, but named Place de la Résistance. It acts as a reminder of the context in which the village wants the novel to be read, no comfort to those who advance its demythologizing status. When I asked in the village and in other parts of the Morvan about reaction to the book, there was universal praise for its portraits of relationships. Repeatedly, people said it was not the reality of the Occupation, but possibly the reality of the Occupation somewhere in a specific place, *la vérité de ce coin-là*. You could not ask for more.

I remember Daniel Aaron's article of 1980 in *Partisan Review* in which he excoriated novelized history as trivializing the past. For him Nathaniel West's *A Cool Million* was "a lunatic novel of the 30s depression," and Robert Coover's *The Public Burning* "a study in the excremental grotesque and a jaundiced version of the Rosenberg case," but he felt obliged to quote Philip Roth's remarks which throw fiction and history into a different light. Modern writers, Roth said in the early 1970s, have their "hands full in trying to understand, and then describe, and then make *credible*, much of the American reality. It stupefies, it sickens, it infuriates, and finally it is a kind of embarrassment to one's imagination. The actuality is continually outdoing our talents, and the culture tosses up figures almost daily that are the envy of any novelist."[7] Historians hear this not as a cry of despair, but as a restatement of the profound, and yet playful, theme that "fact is stranger than fiction." At the same time, the power of simulation and fictional storytelling is a fact in itself.

It must surely be one response to the Némirovsky effect, to affirm this power and to investigate it with the imaginative thinking of which history must be capable.

Nothing is achieved by historians of the Occupation if they are forced onto the defensive by *Suite française*. No reappropriation of reality is achieved by attempts to counteract the merciless pictures of the *exode* and the lyrical portrait of Franco–German relations, or by lists of Némirovsky's omissions, though it is understandable that she should be accused of *mauvaise foi* in her scrabbling for the patronage and protection of the anti-Semitic-right. It is, rather, that the 'Némirovsky effect' is reason for historians to re-engage with the frontiers of fiction and reality, heightened by this astonishing literary product and event, which was a kind of prelude to the equally incredible success of Jonathan Littell's novel *Les Bienveillantes* in 2006, with its memoirs of an all too real, but fictional, SS officer and its musical titles for every section.[8] The historical narratives that are seriously threatened by the impact of either of the novels are only those that are obstinately protected as inviolable.

The challenge posed by the new technology, blogs, and the voices of the net-generation is also an opening to new social evidence, new sources. The perceived threat of reality TV is essential material for research into the complex self-image of today. In French practice, there is a growing respect among contemporary historians for the concept of *l'imaginaire social* (the social imaginary) in which can be situated the impact of every form of fact and fiction on how society views itself.[9]

In these affirmative perspectives, it is necessary to remember that there is a rich consciousness of other comparable material written at the same time as Némirovsky's *Suite française*.

It is *de rigueur* to mention *Le silence de la mer*, the first publication of the clandestine Editions de Minuit in 1942, written by Jean Bruller under the name of Vercors. Némirovsky's Bruno von Falk was compared instantly to the musical German of the Vercors story, Werner von Ebrennac, billeted on a French man and his niece. Both German occupiers were conceived as fiction, or fact. The arrival of the two officers in the novels may be interchangeable, but the message at their departure is not. In a single dramatic twist, Vercors destroyed the image of polite, musical Germans as the reality of the occupiers. Némirovsky left the image intact.

Fewer mentions are made of Jacques Chardonne whose writings in 1940–1 take us in a Vichyite direction. The aristocratic ruralist from the Charente area, a "novelist of intimate feelings," gave a colorful account of a wine-grower's reception of the German colonel billeted on him. They found they had both fought on opposite sides at Verdun. The mutual sympathy, and the wine-grower's best cognac, flowed freely. Chardonne was a liberal notable, not a Nazi sympathiser, but he accepted the Occupation and the billeted German as a tonic for a France he diagnosed as sick: "To cure ourselves," he wrote, "we must learn from our conquerors."[10]

Two among many of the obvious comparisons, Vercors and Chardonne, have often been set alongside each other. The continuing Némirovsky effect, positively engaged, gives the awareness of such parallel writings an extra charge, and accentuates the interaction of fiction and fact as a vast pluralistic area of reality under the Occupation, and particularly central to the history of Resistance. Consider briefly the title given to the hundreds of autobiographical and imaginative gouache paintings done in 1940–2 by the young Charlotte Salomon, Berlin-born Jewish artist, sent by her family to Villefranche, near Nice, where it was thought she would be safe. Seized with her young husband and deported in September 1943, Charlotte was pregnant when she was killed on arrival in Auschwitz. The fictive autobiography of her paintings, all done in France, survived in the hands of a doctor in the Côte d'Azur, but remained unknown until the early 1970s, and were not widely exhibited outside the Jewish Historical Museum of Amsterdam until the late 1990s, their history and content anticipating just a little of the impact of *Suite française*. The title she had given was *Life? or Theater?* and the powerful, personal paintings, full of self-knowledge and human understanding, were accompanied by musical instructions to make the sequence a play with music. Consider also the wryly comic operetta written secretly in Ravensbrück by Germaine Tillion, to keep alive the morale of her fellow prisoners. It was not published until 2005, but was then given a first performance at the Théâtre du Châtelet in June 2007 to mark Germaine Tillion's hundredth birthday. With reference to Offenbach's *Orpheus in the Underworld* it was titled *Le Verfügbar aux Enfers*, "Verfügbar" the name given to those women in Ravensbrück who refused to work, including Tillion herself.[11] Sadly, she could not attend the performance, due to ill health. Nancy Wood, who has written superbly about Tillion and who spent a year working closely with her on her unpublished ethnological writings and photographs of Algeria, was there and movingly described to me the lowering of a vast photograph of Tillion at the end of the performance, at which the whole of the packed theater stood and applauded with tears running down their faces. Tillion had not considered its publication for sixty years, on the basis that it would divert attention from the reality of the suffering. The effect was quite the opposite.

The potency of this mix of simulation and reality must surely continue to produce an emotional reaction, but it also motivates our work on the frontiers of experience and expression. The Occupation as experience is alive and well. Its expression is even more so. I believe it has been strengthened, and not hijacked by the Némirovsky effect, and frontier work on the unexpected and unregarded aspects of the Occupation continues to be done.

The plurality of the Occupation is surely by now inherent in the understanding of the word itself. Paul Virilio in his apocalyptic little portrait of today's urban metropolis, called *Ville panique*, keeps reiterating that "Paris is not all Paris" (*Paris n'est pas tout Paris*).[12] Continuing his logic, "la France" is not all parts of France; "the Occupation" is not all aspects of the Occupation; the singular in each instance obscures and yet contains the plural.

We need fiction to say this with poetry and passion, and it is not a rationalization to argue that the modernist narrative of enlightenment in historical research has come to focus on a plural reality in the last twenty years. It is a logical result of self-awareness.

And this prompts me to one short postscript.

When I returned from Tours in 2004 I was handed an unpublished diary of a young, newly married German-Jewish woman in the Ardèche under the Occupation. The manuscript is now in the German-Jewish archives in the University of Sussex—day by day details of the despair and angry desperation of Kate Haas, not knowing what had happened to her husband, after he had been taken away, apparently only to the nearby town, but in reality to deportation and death. Details too are there, precious details of the people and impulse of rural resistance in that particular area which protected her, throughout the Occupation, from discovery and arrest.

It was that specific image of a Jewish woman, writing feverishly, a demanding and difficult personality, but hidden by a rural community, which shaped much of my first reaction to the Némirovsky event. People did say to me, "How real is *Suite française*?" and there were others, fellow historians, who presumed that because I had worked on resistance as a set of positive narratives, I would be critical of Némirovsky.

I am, but perhaps it is less of a criticism than a final way of responding to the challenge of relating fiction to fact.

So much of real-life resistance activity was a feat of the imagination. In the "Dolce" section of *Suite française*, despite its romance of the masculine, musical German, there is the clearest scenario of how resistance to the occupation often started, even if Némirovsky does not name it as such.

The continued use of his hunting gun by the peasant Benoît, his betrayal to the Germans by the outraged Madame de Montmort who caught him poaching, his impetuous and jealous killing of the German officer Bonnet, his escape across the village, and then the solidarity of the two Angellier women who hide him in their house, using the presence of Bruno von Falk as the best of all covers; this is an imagined event which had real enactments or similarities in the history of resistance in France.

Némirovsky's tragedy, before her arrest and death, was not to have acted on her intuition that resistance to the occupiers could derive from reasons which were neither ideological nor political.[13] Personal obstinacy, reflex action, chance, anger, illegality, pride, and inventiveness were all players in the origin of resistance. Balzac on his deathbed was said to have enquired anxiously about the health and prosperity of characters he had created. I suspect that Némirovsky admired both of the Angellier women she had invented, but not the peasant Benoît, though she gave him some of her best, caustic, lines. Yet, it was he who went into hiding and was hidden, and there's the rub. She may have envisaged herself as one of the Angellier women, hiding others, but could not imagine herself in the role of Benoît.

This is, of course, no more than a hypothesis. But I find there is just this glimpse in the novel's simulation of subterfuge, hiding, and escape, of how the outcome of her own life might have been different. She played imaginatively with everyday life to turn it into fiction. Could she have tried to turn this salient moment of imagination into life?

FIGURE 1 *Preparation of rail sabotage, September 1942.* Photo Apic/Getty Images.

FIGURE 2 *Derailment caused by the Resistance, 1942.* Photo Roger Viollet/Getty Images.

FIGURE 3 *Members of the Resistance listening to a radio message from London, 1940.* Photo Keystone/ Getty Images.

FIGURE 4 *General Charles de Gaulle leaving Downing Street, June 24, 1940. He was recognized by Winston Churchill a few days later on June 28 as "the leader of all the free French who rally to him to defend the allied cause."* Davis/Topical Press Agency/Hulton Archive/ Getty Images.

FIGURE 5 *Jean Moulin (1899–1943). Leading French envoy from de Gaulle and the Free French to the internal Resistance within France, unifier of the Resistance and Founder of the Conseil national de la Résistance (CNR) which first met secretly in Paris on May 27, 1943. He was captured by the Germans at Caluire, outside Lyon, on June 21, 1943, and died as a result of torture in early July of the same year. This photo was taken before the war in 1939 but has been widely used as the iconic image of Moulin, the secret agent.* Corbis/ Getty Images.

FIGURE 6 *Telephone operator at Boussoulet (Haute-Loire, east of Le Puy) informing maquisards of movements of German forces, January 1944.* Getty Images.

FIGURE 7 *Maquisard with gun. Unknown place and date.* Photo -/AFP via Getty Images.

FIGURE 8 *Maquisard in tree with gun. Unknown place and date.* Topfoto.

FIGURE 9 *Farm somewhere in France. This is typical of French scenes under the occupation, widely used by periodicals in London and elsewhere to foster nostalgia for France and identity with resistance against the German Occupation. Many such photos were taken by the famed photographer, Thérèse Bonney, and were extensively featured in* La France Libre *published in London.* Topfoto.

10-12. *These three photos, which are among many procured by Louis Antoine, are kindly provided, together with details, by Louise Bibbey. They feature in the locally-produced, The Maquis d'Ornano. Reports and Testimonies of the Veterans of the Maquis d'Ornano (Tarn- et-Garonne) edited by Élie Molinié, Paul Poussou, Jean Renouard, and the Association of the Maquis d'Ornano, translated by Louise Bibbey.*

FIGURE 10 *A group of the Maquis d'Ornano (Tarn-et-Garonne) in the snow, February 1944. At the front with gun is "Gaby" (Jean Plancke). On the top row from left to right: "Jacques le barbu" (real name unknown); "Loulou" (Jean Renouard); "François" (first name unknown, A maquisard Corse); "Bébert" (Albert Tritschler, killed in the German attack, March 21, 1944); "Léo" (Léo Faerber); "Maxou" (Maurice Delmont).*

FIGURE 11 *Some of the Maquis d'Ornano, who regrouped at Mouillac (Tarn-et-Garonne) March/April 1944, after the German attack. Top row left to right: "Georges" (Élie Molinié); "Charlie" (Otto Braun); "Gérard" (Gérard Ey); "Joë" (René Guillaume). Bottom row: "Pierre" (Pierre Broggi); "Yves" (Bruno Munaretto); "Loulou" (Jean Renouard); "Le Sabre" (Henri Castejon).*

FIGURE 12 *Lucienne Baudé ("Sim"), village schoolteacher in Mouillac, described as "one of the most courageous figures of the resistance" by the Veterans of the Maquis d'Ornano.*

13-15. These three photos have been kindly provided, together with details, by Alan Latter and come from two albums he has created in research and writing on resistance activity in the south west of France, notably on the maquisards of the Brigade Rac in the north of the Dordogne, as featured here. All three photos were taken by a local photographer, André Léonard, who was part of the maquis, in the Boudeau forest near Thiviers (Dordogne). Alan Latter's website is given among others at the end of the Bibliography, below

FIGURE 13 *A maquisard of the Brigade Rac singing to others at the table, May 1944.*

FIGURE 14 *A maquisard of the Brigade Rac preparing for an ambush, May 1944.*

FIGURE 15 *Maquisards of the Brigade Rac, at the table with three Allied airmen, who parachuted from their Halifax plane, before it crashed after dropping containers of arms to the Resistance at Brive (Corrèze). Flight Sergeant E. Jones (British), is raising a glass; Flight Sergeant Harold Blackett (British) is sitting on the other side of the table, next to the man in the foreground; and Flight Officer R. Evans (Canadian) is sitting two places beyond Sgt. Jones, May 1944.*

FIGURE 16 *Resistance fighters at a Paris window, August 1944.* Topfoto.

FIGURE 17 *Resisters at their underground headquarters in the Paris catacombs, August 1944.* Topfoto.

FIGURE 18 *Liberation of Paris. Smiling resister, August 1944.* Topfoto.

FIGURE 19 *Ex-resisters, Lucie and Raymond Aubrac at home. Paris 1990s. See Chapter 3, The Aubrac Affair, above.* Getty Images.

FIGURE 20 *Hubert Germain, ex-resister with the Free French, and later a Député for Paris 14e and a Gaullist Minister in the early 1970s, photographed, aged 100, as the last surviving member of Les Compagnons de la Libération, at the funeral of Daniel Cordier, Hôtel des Invalides, Paris, November 26, 2020.* Getty Images.

7

Commemoration and Testimony

The variables of place will always be a necessary leitmotif in resistance research and testimony, as, indeed, they were in the lived history of resistance, with a variety of starting points and places in 1940 through to a Liberation which is dated at different times for different places. The variables of place are inseparable from the variables of time. Both are structural to the way we explore the diversity of Resistance. Places acknowledged in history all become places of new discovery in the present and the future.

In 2010 the seventieth anniversary of de Gaulle's first broadcast to France on the BBC was celebrated by both French and British historians who deliberately foregrounded London in a week of commemorative events.

London, in the words of French historian Robert Frank, can be firmly defined as "Un haut-lieu de la résistance française," a prime site, center, and epic progenitor of French resistance. To be accurate, Frank's words denoted "L'Angleterre," England, not London, but all the details and references in his article in the invaluable *Dictionnaire historique de la Résistance*, edited by François Marcot, refer to London. It was the capital, he wrote, of the only country in 1940 to repel the German assault, the capital of governments in exile, and, as he put it, "the European capital of Resistances" in the plural.[1]

Those who investigate the attitudes of British people in 1940 to the French, de Gaulle, and Anglo-French relations, often start with a wealth of evidence in the grassroots material collected by Mass-Observation, founded in 1937 by Tom Harrisson, a self-trained anthropologist, the poet Charles Madge, and the filmmaker Humphrey Jennings. Its voluminous archive is now held at the University of Sussex. Historians and program-makers are regularly researching this amazing archive, but we still do not know if public opinion in Yorkshire or Suffolk or anywhere else was more supportive of French resistance than opinion in any other county or region. Nobody has asked that question as yet, and perhaps there would be no credible answer if we did, but access to knowledge of secret houses and secret training across Britain has grown exponentially since the late 1980s. The intricate relationships between the different secret bodies excite more questions than can probably be answered, but the zeal to discover the places where they operated, and the personnel and activities involved, is now a staple of local history.

Enticingly, there is the little autobiographical booklet by Barbara Bertram called, *French Resistance in Sussex*, about her house in Bignor, used secretly to accommodate French resisters and special agents en route to or from France, with a Foreword by Hugh Verity, that incomparable pilot of Lysanders, who flew on night flights into France to rival any Saint-Exupéry novel.[2]

Through the testimony of Brooks Richards we have detailed evidence of maritime resistance organized secretly from notable country houses in the Helford estuary in Cornwall. Ever since reading the meticulous insights in his *Secret Flotillas* and interviewing him in his home I have wanted to research the stories of those Cornish houses, creeks, and inlets. He himself wanted a few Francophile plaques in Cornwall to say "It happened here."

There is already one in Falmouth and will hopefully be one soon in Newlyn, the major fishing port west of Penzance, after the boost provided in February 2010 by an article in the Newlyn Fishing News, published on the internet as *Through the Gaps*. It pointed to the seventieth anniversary of 1940 and gave new evidence of Newlyn's close involvement with resistance refugees and volunteers from the ports of Brittany. One of the trawlers which was given both refuge and work in Newlyn was suitably called the "Entente Cordiale."

The Secret WW2 Learning Network, created as a charity and educational organization by Martyn Cox and Martyn Bell in the southeast of the United Kingdom, promotes a countrywide rediscovery of places where training and operations fuelled intelligence gathering and subversion "behind enemy lines" whether in Europe or the Far East. Largely exploring and expanding the underground history of the SOE and its infrastructure, it creates social and educational events which set out to reveal sites and involvement on both sides of the Channel. Featuring audiovisual testimonies recorded and edited by Martyn Cox and the expansive research and perceptive writings of the military historian Paul McCue, the network has recently secured the local placing of blue plaques to commemorate individual SOE agents and agency. Both the surprise and involvement they engender is a reminder of how memory thrives if it is localized and enabled by dedicated resources. This dedication has been the explicit aim of David Harrison's uniquely sensitive venture over more than thirty years to help those, often family members or descendants, with research into the hidden lives of SOE agents. His forthcoming, and even more original, database will go further and provide details of some fifteen thousand French people who were locally involved in more than eighty SOE circuits within France.

Many of the rigorous, technical training sites for SOE agents scheduled for action in Occupied Europe were located in northern England, Wales, and Scotland, while further to the north the local pride of the Shetland Islanders in their operations with the SOE and the Norwegian Resistance foregrounds yet another vital secret history of fishing communities, presented in the North Sea museum in Shetland at Scalloway. It documents and celebrates the boats which brought back resisters and refugees from Norway in dangerous operations and were nicknamed collectively "The Shetland Bus," and the eventual major success of resistance sabotage in the destruction of the hydroelectric plant at Vemork, preventing the production of heavy water needed by Nazi Germany for the creation of an atomic bomb.[3]

Returning to London, there is not only the equivalence of London and Britain implied by Robert Frank, but equally the identification of London with the BBC, known to those listening in France as "Radio Londres" or "La voix de Londres." Widely acknowledged by historians as a catalyst for organized resistance, the BBC also addressed itself directly to those Jean-Louis Crémieux-Brilhac identified as the "unorganised mass of resisters and sympathisers."[4]

Equally redolent of London's centrality to resistance was the comment by André Labarthe, the founder, with Raymond Aron, of the London monthly review, La France Libre. "Sometimes," he wrote, "we can see France shining like a mirage at the end of a London street." Alongside its essays, the review published evocative photos of French provincial towns and rural scenes and, above all, Paris. They carried their own imperative: the personal as well as the national necessity of liberation. Not the least of London's achievements was to foster a nostalgia for France in the true sense of the term in which the Greek word "nostos" means return. The anguish of the need to return led the French exiles to a remarkable set of resistance actions on the one hand and to the post-Liberation continuities on the other, as discussed in Chapter 4.

Within France itself, the diversity of place and resistance is increasingly theorized and researched. It is now a mosaic of ideas and conclusions, marking the impact of the six major conferences on La Résistance et les Français staged across the 1990s. The relativity of place is thriving, in MA dissertations, doctorates, monographs, and conference papers, and with it the stress on the variables of time, personality, motivation, class, politics, race, and gender.

This diversity needs to be accessible. It is, increasingly so, as more and more localities in France prioritize their own heritage, terrain, culture, and political and social structures, in the way they present the local history of resistance. Urban or rural, this recognition of local history now accompanies most new research on resistance. The work done on Lille and the Nord-Pas-de-Calais, for example, stresses the high level of pro-British sentiment, specific to the area and dating from the First World War, which became a widespread motivating force for resistance. I myself was first struck by the questions of place when I visited Brive in the Corrèze in the early 1970s, site of Edmond Michelet's act of refusal on June 17, 1940, immediately after hearing Pétain's speech calling for a cease-fire. His typed statements of defiance, taken from the writings of Charles Péguy and distributed to people in the street, have become almost as legendary locally as de Gaulle's first "Appel" at the national level. When I asked "Why Michelet?" I was met with one response from a local resister, saying, "Why Brive?" His own answer was specific: there had been a strong local pocket of sympathy for the Spanish Republican exiles and refugees in 1939.

Combining archives and memory, there are now a substantial number of new or re-organized local museums of resistance and travel books in which resistance is strikingly chronicled and situated. For example, on the edge of the Île de France, lies the little-known area of the Gâtinais, where the strategic importance of canals, locks, and rivers determined the actions of resistance. Here there is a superb little booklet and guide to the dispersed sites of small groups of resisters, and exact details of how to discover where and how they were active, the area still replete with informed local memory. In its own microrural way, it rivals the street by street, place by place guide to resistance in Paris, published by Parigramme in 2007.[5]

In the collective and individual memory of resistance, it is not only named places, but often a particular space that carries the weight of what was essentially a clandestine and minority history: a cellar, the back room of a café, a landing field, a bookshop, a bridge or street corner, a letter box, a railway carriage, the inside of a prison, a wall on which to paint a victory V or a cross of Lorraine, a shepherd's hut in which to hide, the safe or embattled spaces in forests and on plateaux and hills, the clandestine routes crossing the demarcation line, the narrow alleys, steps, and connecting passages, *ruelles, traboules and dédales*, in southern towns, so vital for understanding the possibilities of resistance in Lyon, for example. We can accurately situate the first resistance activities of Agnès Humbert in Paris in 1940 from the places and spaces described so precisely in the diary which opens her memoir *Notre Guerre*. Her group came to be known by the name of the place in which it originated, the Musée de l'Homme (the museum of humankind). As a movement, it was the center of a constellation of very small groups, each identified by place, a practice which became widespread in the later period of the maquis. Humbert's astonishing memoir has been skillfully edited in English by Barbara Mellor, and is given the title of the group's newspaper, *Résistance*, the first clandestine publication to carry the word as a title of individual and collective reactions of refusal and revolt.[6]

When I had finished Matthew Cobb's narrative of the liberation of Paris, published in 2013, I felt as if I knew every barricade and every street fighter by name, and every hour of those dramatic eleven days by its specific twists, turns, hopes, and conflicts. On every page it brings actions and decisions at the top into subtle counterpoint with decisions and actions from below in smoke-filled rooms, hidden courtyards, cafes, and the labyrinth of Paris streets. Historical polyphony at its best brings spontaneous and calculated civilian resistance together with high-level military strategy. In summary,

> the liberation of Paris . . . was about the ordinary people of Paris who rose up against the Germans and made it impossible for the Allies to pursue their intended policy of skirting round the city. The population did not liberate the city single-handed, but their courage and sacrifice changed the situation, while the advance of the Allied armies not only gave the population the confidence that overwhelming force would soon be on their side, but also forced the surrender of the German garrison. In its final stage the liberation of Paris was a joint operation between the Resistance, the Leclerc Division and the Americans.[7]

As I read this, I switched back to one of the key quotes in the book. Jean Guéhenno, cultural Europeanist, editor of the periodical *Europe,* and lycée professor of literature, allowed himself a moment of lyricism on the evening of August 21, 1944: "Liberty is returning," he wrote in his diary.

> We don't know where it is, but it is out there, all around us in the night. It is coming with the armies. We feel immensely grateful. It is the most profound joy to realise that all you have thought about people is true. We cannot break our chains alone. But all free men are marching together. They are here.[8]

The trope of "night," like that of "shadows" in Kessel's *Armée des Ombres* (Shadow Army) written in 1943, and before that, the metaphor of "silence" in *Le silence de la mer* (Silence of the sea) written a year earlier by Vercors, and the pantheism of *liberté,* as used by Eluard and Guéhenno are all grand evocative words, steeped in cultural resonance, and widely used at the time to convey the "esprit" or character of Resistance. They were and, to a large extent, remain the preferred way of representing resistance, allowing it to establish a cultural presence in twentieth-century history. Turning to the original of the Guéhenno diary, he continued the day's entry in the same literary vein: " Grand words," he writes, "are true words. . . . We have learned this from every hardship and ordeal, even though my hand still trembles in the act of writing them down."[9]

Today there is a recognition of the need to interrogate and understand the role played by such language alongside the ever-present need for more comparative and empirical research.

Over the last seventy years the study of resistance has always struggled to establish itself alongside the study of war and the study of revolution, the two mainstream ways of investigating historical conflict and major historical turning points. We have now left that situation behind. There is not only a wealth of meticulous new research on civilian resistance and on the infrastructure of special forces but also a great range of new empirical material on the nature and impact of unacceptable occupation. Resistance in France was always a minority phenomenon, and at the start a scattered and diffuse minority. Motivation and choice have become keywords in assessing the small numbers of civilians who first formed isolated clusters of resistance. In this flowering of new research, what has been retained is the presence of the literary, cultural, and ethical dimensions of resistance. They have not been jettisoned in a competitive, instrumental argument about effectiveness. The more research develops and the more it expands into legacy and historiography, the more it has to take on board the role of words, grand words, as an active constituent of resistance.

The revolutionary year of 1989 in Eastern Europe resurrected the study of revolutions, but anyone researching the collapse of the Soviet Union or the contemporary collapse of apartheid in South Africa could not fail to register the creative role played over years and years by little-known resistance groups, whether in Russian clandestine jazz clubs, or Czech underground theater, or in the illegal gatherings which led to the African National Congress. Comparative resistance history is not just an academic exercise but a feature of everyday political discussion, and media revelations.

Oral transmission of history from one generation to another continues to take place with or without the presence of a historian. History continues to be written with or without oral testimonies. It is vital to bring these two processes together, affirming that people have their own history to tell, and that both interviewer and interviewee will benefit.

Whatever it may, or may not, add to historical knowledge, oral testimony will always do two things: it will give an individual the chance to be the subject, or the author of his/her own history, and second, it will at the very least suggest hypotheses which the historian can further investigate. Both of these things enhance the very nature and value of researching and writing history. It healthily diversifies the answer to the critical question, "Whose history is it anyway?"

Textual testimony, such as diaries and intimate journals, sets a benchmark for oral testimony. Take Hélène Berr's self-awareness of her role in keeping a diary of the horrific persecution and deportation of her Jewish friends in Paris and, eventually, of her own Jewish family. She argues that she has to write it down as her own act of refusal, revolt, and resistance, and she does so more and more angrily until she herself is deported to her death. Without saying it exactly, she was acknowledging a "devoir de raconter" (duty to recount as it is happening), anticipating the much later, postwar demands of a "devoir de mémoire" (duty of remembering). Her *Journal*, prefaced by Patrick Modiano, is one of the most moving and compulsive literary products of the Occupation. Her resistance to the spreading tentacles of the Holocaust is her story.[10]

* * *

Several people in the Cahors area in the département of the Lot told me that I must meet Simone Conquet who had been involved in acts of resistance from start to finish and continued after the war. She was widely referred to as "the teacher of English." I interviewed her on March 22, 1991.

Mlle. Simone CONQUET

My own village was just over the river Lot from Saint-Cirq-Lapopie, called Tour-de-Faure. My mother and sister died of Spanish flu just before the end of the First World War. When my father came back from the war I was only four and I remember what an emotional meeting it was at the station. There were Russian prisoners of war, taken after the Russian Revolution, and they were very kind to me. So, too, were all my father's fellow workers at the brickworks. I think that kindness was very important to me, because when I became a schoolteacher it seemed natural to help Jewish refugees after the defeat. I was at the College of Montluc and I sheltered the young son of the Jewish editor at Gallimard Publishing. I didn't do much but he was grateful.

I knew about the *réfractaires* and tried to encourage one of my colleagues not to leave for STO. I was very surprised when he said he would go. And then there was one *réfractaire* who was hidden in a cave in my village. The others fed him. He went off to a maquis but didn't like it much and came back into hiding.

In 1943 I was teaching English in the College at Cahors. It was then that I started taking messages to the villages outside Cahors. Not all the peasants were in favor of the maquis. At the Liberation, letters of denunciation were found at the Préfecture. There was one I remember which said, "I am a farmer in the Ségala. I fought in the First World War and am a loyal French citizen. There is a maquis unit in the woods opposite my farm." It was signed with a full address. It was difficult to believe. When I went round the area I was often surprised at the absence of security. It often seemed to be fairly chaotic. I cycled everywhere and was never arrested. I had to bluff my way through police blocks going out of Cahors and coming back. Sometimes I went by train, arriving back after the curfew, but I always got a pass from the authorities at the station. I suppose technically I was a liaison agent for the clandestine Liberation Committee in Cahors, and one of the two or three women on the committee at the Liberation, alongside Madame Lurçat. I was also involved in social care for the families of resisters and deportees. When the deportees returned from the camps, I was one of those who helped them to resettle. I can never forget the distress: it was terrible. The things they had suffered. When I was offered a Resistance medal I said, "Give it to those who have suffered so much." I wasn't religious but I was deeply affected by it all. I wasn't a feminist really: it just seemed human decency to do something. And I did nothing compared with someone like the police officer at the Cahors gendarmerie, Commandant Vessières, who sheltered Jews and resisters and did so much for Cahors Resistance, or Madame Lurçat whose courage as a liaison agent was enormous, or, of course, Jean-Jacques Chapou: he was such a great leader.[11]

A stream of local names flowed from most interviews with ex-resisters: it nourished further travels, new meetings, and more archival research. The readiness to acknowledge the role of others was in itself a confident sign of authenticity: the other people named could be asked to authenticate the testimony given. Ownership and accounts of resistance activity in these interviews is rarely an exercise in egoism. The SOE agent, Francis Cammaerts, who has been mentioned several times in previous chapters, made this abundantly clear on March 18, 1991, at his home in the southeast département of the Drôme. This is a short extract from a long interview.

Francis CAMMAERTS

Without the women there could have been no Resistance. In my whole time in France I never slept in a hotel. I stayed only in people's houses, with their families. The women looked after the grandparents, the children, and us. And every day they went off on a bicycle with a trailer in search of food. What needs emphasis is the role of women, and children, in the security of the Resistance. I never heard of a single person who had been put in danger by a child's indiscretion. Take Madame Reynier for example, in Crest, with whom I was staying at one point. She was arrested by the Vichy Milice with her three children. They were all stripped naked and questions were fired at them about the whereabouts of her husband and myself. She seemed a timid little woman, but she just kept saying how her husband ran around with other women. She stuck to her story, and eventually they gave her back her clothes and sent her home. Wonderful courage; and it's almost a banal story: it was not an exceptional event.[12]

Harry Rée, fellow SOE agent and friend, whose resistance actions in the Jura region became equally legendary in postwar local memory, was always anxious to play down his own achievements and leadership. His son, Jonathan Rée, has brilliantly researched and edited his father's written testimonies and broadcasts, in which the roles and tragedies of named local families are movingly prioritized.[13]

There was also, in many oral testimonies, a personal need to correct a particular story and reveal truths that had been, and still were, occluded. When Madeleine Baudoin in Marseille insisted that I had to listen to the testimony of Joseph Pastor, it was for this reason. I met him on September 13, 1971.

M. Joseph PASTOR

I was forty-seven in 1940 and was, by training, an engineer, though because of my communist ideas I did not want to be caught in a factory between employers and workers, so I became self-employed. I lived in Marseille and was married, with two children. Since 1930 I had been a member of the Communist Party, though in the 1930s I was already critical of the party for failing to become genuinely revolutionary. All it could do was follow Stalin's wishes. The Nazi–Soviet pact was part of Stalin's determination to look after Russian interests at all costs, but although I rejected the pact I stayed in the party. I was mobilized at the start of the war only to be imprisoned as a "notorious communist and propagandist who must be locked up."

I tried to contact the party at the end of January 1940 but found no trace of it. It had disappeared after being dissolved but not before condemning me for my critical attitude to the Nazi–Soviet pact. I started, therefore, to reconstruct the party in the south of Marseille among my old comrades. Some, who rejected me, had little concern to restart the party and made no attempt to stay hidden. As a result many were arrested.

By August 1940 I had reconstituted the party in my area of Marseille, and in that month a senior party official from Montpellier was sent to contact me. In good faith I duly passed on all my information and gave him the names of my comrades. A month later I was arrested. A Vichy police spy had penetrated the very heart of the organization and used my documents to destroy the party. When I heard this I escaped from my internment camp. As soon as I was free, the Vichy police circulated a rumor that it was I who had betrayed all my comrades. The party believed the stories. They were still opposed to me because of my attitude to the Nazi–Soviet pact. They at once said I was a Vichy spy in the pay of the police.

I came back clandestinely to Marseille, and began again to construct a group, this time only among comrades who shared my views. We were about thirty and we brought out about five or six numbers of the local party paper *Rouge-Midi* in 1941, calling for sabotage of material going to Germany and for the formation of a front against the occupiers. These proposals were condemned by the party in its own numbers of *Rouge-Midi*.

Between 1940 and 1942 there was virtually no resistance in Marseille except for a few individuals and small groups. Among the workers, this was due to the rivalry between Communists and Socialists and the fact that there were very few militants among them. A militant is someone who is born that way. One is a fighter by nature. For that reason there was no merit in being a resister: one was there by nature. There were many jobs and professions represented in the Resistance simply because it was a question of character, not politics.

I avoided capture but was under sentence of death by Vichy proclamation, while the Communist Party continued to call for my death, calling me a police agent. Eventually I was responsible for bringing the party in Marseille into contact with three movements of resistance, Combat, Libération, and Franc-Tireur, in a meeting in my clandestine hiding place. This was done without telling the party that I was the one behind the meeting. But I was there, listening from the kitchen.[14]

8

A Generic Conclusion

The powerful mythical language of good and bad is visible in the medieval dooms of heaven and hell over many a chancel arch in local village churches. I first looked at these dooms when I was a student in the late 1950s. At that time it was normal to see these mythical statements and lament the absence of such myths in the twentieth century. Rosenberg's 1930 *Myth of the Twentieth Century* was discounted as a polemic for Nazism, and the language of historical analysis did not include the word "mythopoeic."

Roland Barthes had just written *Mythologies* (1957) but it was little known. Myths meant the legends of antiquity as brilliantly retold in 1955 by Robert Graves, who was himself a bit of a legend when we backed him in Oxford for Professor of Poetry in 1961, a campaign memorable for the placards which read "We dig Graves."

Since then, slowly and then precipitously, we have descended, or ascended, into a world where everything can possibly be seen as a myth. Discovering myths, inventing myths, using the concept of mythification, recoding every event or personality in terms of myth, has become an intellectual and even pedagogical reflex. To the statement that "I'm working on the camaraderie of the trenches in World War One" comes the inevitable reply, "you mean the myth of camaraderie." Asked for a suitable subtitle for a biographical study of Jean Moulin, the resistance hero whose ashes were transferred to the Panthéon in 1964, or for the life of General de Gaulle, the predictable suggestion is "Man and Myth." And the "myth of resistance" is everywhere.

Myths to the historian are now as central as stories were to Trevelyan. Excitingly, they are often the first step of the political historian toward cultural history.

Resisters in France were a minority, but the popular identification with the Liberation in 1944, superbly captured in the Chadwyck-Healey collection at Cambridge, is one of an enormous majority, with ideas, imagery, concepts, legends, and myths from a wealth of sources, suggesting a surprisingly extensive meaning of what the Liberation, the endgame of resistance, was all about.

For years after de Gaulle's declaration on August 25, 1944, down to today, many historians, and particularly British and American ones, dismissed the general's formulation as "the Gaullist myth" or quite simply as "the French myth." The most that these historians concede is that this mythmaking had the aim of uniting France after four years of calamitous, dark and divisive events, and as such the liberational myth was functional, instrumental, and largely successful. The problem is that the perpetual reference to "the Gaullist myth" as untrue has become a rigid and unimaginative block on the understanding of the role that myths were already playing at the time, well before the Liberation.

A myth of France liberated by itself, by a popular uprising, by its own struggle, by its own armies, was certainly created at the Liberation, but powerful myths of such an outcome were already there, empowering resistance actions and ideas, and enabling a much wider cross-section of French people, in 1944, to feel they were part of the liberational story.

The myth and legends of popular action had a long pedigree in French history in accounts of the barricades in the streets of Paris at the Revolution of 1789 and at all subsequent revolutionary moments in the nineteenth century, and in the pervading notions of a citizen army made legendary by the victory over the Prussians at Valmy on September 20, 1792, which led to the proclamation of the First Republic.

In September 1940, on the anniversary day of that legendary victory, a teacher of French at the Lycée Buffon in Paris, Raymond Burgard, formed a pioneer movement against the Armistice and the Occupation, which he named Valmy, made up of young Catholic Democrats and veterans of the First World War, including Paulin Bertrand, known by his *nom de guerre* Paul Simon. In December 1941 Simon crossed to London to join de Gaulle. There he began a tour of lectures featuring the clandestine movement and publication *Valmy*, which he made into the book, *Un seul ennemi, l'envahisseur* (*One Enemy Only–the Invader*), to which I alluded in Chapter 1. His lectures can really be called the first testimony on the origins and growth of a particular resistance movement inside France with a direct reference to a legendary revolutionary event.

Myths underlying resistance action should be known as *réalités mentales*, realities of the mind. They are legendary experiences or memories which acquire a motivating force. The seven-volume project on national memory in the 1980s by Pierre Nora, *Les lieux de mémoire* (Realms of Memory), made it clear that events in the past remain an active force in shaping attitudes and lives in the present, and he included in this the enduring significance of certain French places, people, rituals, and objects in forming a set of realities of the mind, not unlike the elusive but evocative taste of the madeleine in Marcel Proust's pursuit of time lost but remembered.

An influential early resister in the Free French circles in London, and then historian of the whole Gaullist movement, Jean-Louis Crémieux-Brilhac recognized immediately that de Gaulle and La France Libre were both reality and myth in the minds of the Occupied French, and he continued to emphasize this combination throughout his writings. The coexistence of the two, he claimed, was recognized by de Gaulle whom he described as the "knowing artisan of them both" (l'artisan conscient de l'un et de l'autre).[1]

In the dark days of the Occupation there were memories and myths which acquired an extra potency when travel and distances returned to a preindustrial timescale, when communities were thrown back onto local possibilities and references. Find these myths, locate them, look at their power to motivate, and you begin to give resistance its diffuse cultural and historical dimensions.

In the beautiful, austere, wooded, and mountainous Cévennes, the southeasterly terrain of the Massif central, the potent memory of the early eighteenth-century revolt of Protestant Huguenots, known locally as Camisards, who defied Louis XIV's revocation of religious freedom, was handed down by stories told from generation to generation, an oral process brilliantly analyzed by Philippe Joutard in 1977 as La Légende des Camisards: une sensibilité au passé (The legend of the Camisards: a sensibility to the past).

Already specified previously, in Chapter 2, the legend made the peasant Camisard fighters into heroes, victims, and martyrs, and was widened by the memory of the persecution of Protestants both before and after the revolt. It was in 1730, twenty years after the apparent end of the Camisard revolt, that the eighteen-year-old Protestant Marie Durand was arrested and subjected to what became thirty-eight years of cruel incarceration in the Tour de Constance in the fortified provençal town of Aigues-Mortes. On the wall of her prison, she wrote the word Résister.

Two hundred years later, under the German Occupation, the Cévennes lived up to its mythic reputation as the land of revolt and refuge, as a stubborn and principled region where those pursued and victimized by the Germans or Vichy would be taken in and protected. The marching song of one of the maquis units, La Soureilhade, which is Occitan for "Sunlit," had as its refrain, "In the veins of the maquisards flows the pure blood of the Camisards."

Toward the Pyrenees in the Ariège, there was a widespread folk memory which persisted after the so-called Guerre des Demoiselles (War of the young women) in 1829. Male peasants had taken to the woods disguised in women's clothes in a revolt against a law restricting access to state and private forests. This association of "access to forests," "popular protest," and "dissimulation" was reawakened early after the defeat of 1940, when small local groups in the Ariège organized the first escape routes over the mountains taking British airmen, Poles, and Czechs, often heavily disguised, through forests and across the frontier. François Rouan was one of these early *passeurs*, people who passed them across. He told me in 1982 that they were a movement of anti-fascist Resistance, grouping together immigrant miners, construction and forestry workers, all very ordinary men. He added, "We were outlaws already and I was completely clandestine, living in miserable circumstances from hand to mouth."[2] Local legends of outlaw figures were widely prevalent in many areas, at a time when national issues took on form and meaning in local terms. "What group of resisters," wrote the regional historian Paul Silvestre, "did not seek to identify itself with some hero from local folklore . . . or from the national pantheon of revolutionaries . . . potent images of hope?"[3]

The clandestine publications of resistance writers were full of "realities of the mind," not least reclaiming the legendary Joan of Arc from the clerical and anti-English propaganda of Vichy. The works of the poet Paul Eluard were especially vital in the creative role of resistance. One of the leading lights of Surrealism from the early 1920s, and a humanist communist, Eluard was a close friend of André Breton, Max Ernst, Man Ray, Salvador Dali, Louis Aragon, and Pablo Picasso, dedicated to using poetry to bring people together, to inspire and enlighten relationships, social commitment, and political engagement. In 1939, he wrote, "Poetry only becomes flesh and blood when it is reciprocal"—that is, bringing people together.

In 1942 a love poem by Eluard, written in the summer of 1941 and called "Une seule pensée" (One Single Thought), found its way through Switzerland to Algeria, where it was printed by the Literary magazine *Fontaine*. Each of the twenty stanzas ends with the refrain, "I write your name," presumably the name of Maria Benz who became known as Nusch and was Eluard's passionately loved, second wife. Tantalizingly, her name is withheld, as he writes it on every object from school desk to trees, on clouds, sand, snow, the seasons, the horizon, the wings of birds, on fruit cut in two, on the forehead of friends, on places of refuge, on ruins, on absence and on solitude, on the steps of death, on every outstretched hand. Finally in the very last word, the name is revealed: "I was born to know you, to name you . . . 'Liberté.'"

Its affective imagery made the poem immediately relevant to the lives of people creating the Resistance. It was printed and reprinted clandestinely, with "Liberté" as its new title. It was read in small gatherings all over France after it was dropped in thousands of copies by the R. A. F. The master tapestry artist, Jean Lurçat, working secretly in a workshop at Aubusson, produced a tapestry version in 1943.

This was liberty in words to match the famous painting by Delacroix of "Liberty leading the people" on the barricades of 1830, her Phrygian bonnet the legendary headwear of revolutionaries, symbol of revolt and civilization, recalling the mythic heroism of the Phrygian people against the Hittite Empire in northern Greece in the twelfth century BCE.

Eluard's poem, in the course of two years, achieved a comparable mythic status. Liberty in the poem is a tangible presence, touching all things experienced and imagined in the everyday life of the Occupation. This reincorporation of everything that was life-affirming was central to the literature of resistance.

A year after the Liberation, Eluard looked back to the fact that the Germans had threatened to destroy the bridges of Paris, and he wrote, "No one can destroy the bridges which lead us to sleep and from sleep to our dreams, and from our dreams to eternity. Enduring city where I have lived our victory over death." This celebrates the truly mythic nature of the Liberation, not so much de Gaulle's formulation on August 25, 1944, but this claim to "our victory over death" ("notre victoire sur la mort"): poetry as flesh and blood, reciprocal, bringing people together. The Liberation did just that, in the same way that Eluard's poem had suggested two years earlier, by universalizing the tangible presence of liberty with which whole sections of French society could readily identify.

What is significant today is for us to interrogate the very phrase used by Eluard, "notre victoire sur la mort." As I've just presented it, it seems to confirm that Eluard was speaking for everyone, "our victory." In one sense he was.

But we know he was disillusioned by the way in which the Liberation allowed many French people to jump on the Resistance bandwagon, to dig out their moth-eaten uniforms from the First World War and parade themselves as heroes, people who became derisively known by active resisters as *les naphtalinards,* literally the "mothballers." The Liberation as event did allow everyone to feel an identity with Liberté, but "our victory over death" in Eluard's meaning was far more specific. It was the claim of those who had taken on the occupiers, who had rebelled and resisted in their everyday lives, who had, indeed, been confronted by the constant threat and actuality of torture and death.

The memoirs and statements of resisters abound with specific definitions of "our" war, the war with which their lives were associated. The mobilization of myths and legends, some national, some very local, was the achievement of an active minority, with its own self-awareness of the struggle it involved. Only ultimately was it a mobilization that permitted a wide public identification with the spirit of Liberation.

Most of the pioneers of the Musée de l'Homme network, close colleagues, comrades, and friends of Agnès Humbert, were arrested and executed in 1941, and she herself was deported to Germany where she survived slave working conditions over two terrible years. That was what she meant by "our war" in her memoir *Notre Guerre.*

Jacques Debû-Bridel, one of the leaders of the literary and intellectual resistance in Paris, a co-founder of the clandestine Éditions de Minuit, wrote that "The war that we were fighting was more than a national war. It was a war of principle, of ideas." That was their war.[4]

We talk a lot about the totality of war in the twentieth century, far less about the specificity of war. One of the first necessities of research into resistance is to confront specific places, specific motivations, and specific lives.

Unlike conscription in warfare, resistance was voluntary and uncharted. Every tactic or strategy had to be invented, such as seeing yourself as a potential intelligence agent: the Germans were there in your streets and in your houses and you could make spying your daily activity. Forging identity cards in a local town hall demanded no less ingenuity than guerrilla activity in the woods. Error and failure were catastrophic for individuals and families; but success also could trigger the retaliation of devastating and brutal German reprisals on the surrounding community.

Art historian, Jean Cassou, famously called his refusal *un refus absurde,* meaning it flew in the face of everything that was deemed at the time to be rational and realistic. He was an individual who thought at once about myths and legendary precedents. In August 1940 he and Agnès Humbert discussed what to do against the occupation, and talked of forming a group of people who shared their mentality of refusal. "A group like the Carbonari?" he suggested.

Formed as a secret political society in early nineteenth-century Italy, the Carbonari became a part-mythical European movement against any form of tyranny. Mazzini, Byron, Lafayette, and the French socialist Auguste Blanqui were all said to be members. It took much of its organization and its secret signs from republican Freemasonry and entered into French literature through Stendhal's short story of love and revolt written in 1829, *Vannina Vannini.* Cassou easily imagined the international group of resistance forming round the Musée de l'Homme in Paris as a reincarnation.

By contrast, Madeleine Baudoin, whom I interviewed in Marseille not long after the 1968 student revolt, claimed that her refusal in 1940 was ahead of its time by some twenty-eight years. She had been, she said, *une gauchiste avant le mot* (a left-wing activist well before the term was common). She was still a fiery person at age forty-seven when she arranged to meet me in a local café at 10:00 a.m. I arrived early with my tape recorder, which at the time was a Uher, a large reel-to-reel machine. A collection of men in their working *blousons* were at the bar drinking their first, second, or third pastis of the day. I thought I had better do the same, but, as I ordered, the other drinkers began to move closer to me, eyeing my tape recorder in its leather bag. Worried about losing it before I had even met Mlle Baudoin, I started to edge toward the door. At that moment she arrived, and I quickly mumbled what I was doing. Sweeping me back into the café, she said, "They knew you were coming; they all want to be part of the recording."

Later on, by contrast, she made her sense of isolation in 1940 into the core of her testimony. "To stand out," she said, "and to resist, by wanting to go on fighting against the Germans was like living in a foreign country." "Even in Marseille?" I asked. "Yes, even in Marseille."

The same self-identity as an exception marks most of the lives and testimonies of resisters, however much they claimed to embody France as a whole. This apparent anomaly is central to an understanding of French resistance. Both exception and embodiment are coupled throughout. It was their claim to authenticity. Yes, they were illegal, but yes, they were legitimate. Therein lies the creativity of resistance lives.

The map of resistance across France in 1940–2 has been likened to a map of the night sky, showing clusters of stars, nebula, constellations. These words are now regularly used, particularly by Julien Blanc who has brought to life the nebula of small groups across the north of France who made up the early resistance of the Musée de l'Homme network. Creating a cluster was itself the first act of resistance: finding others who could be trusted, at a time when the prewar political map was in tatters.

Writing for an English publication just after the Liberation, Jean-Paul Sartre wrote a piece called "Paris under the Occupation." He rightly stresses the impossibility of knowing what it was like to be occupied unless you had experienced it. But his references to resistance are vague and nonspecific. Penetrating questions of who, what, when, and where were not immediately asked. A degree of continued secrecy about resistance details, combined with ignorance about them, pervaded the postliberation scene.

There was, however, an immediate acceptance at the Liberation of the idea of resistance as *L'armée des ombres* (army of the shadows). Some representations of this in the Chadwyck-Healey collection are particularly significant. One particular drawing by Jean-Louis Chancel, a professional illustrator and a resistance leader of an intelligence network in the south of France, is titled simply *Résistance*, and subtitled *L'armée des ombres*, evoking nightmares and dreams, and imaging a web or network of ghostly shadows encircling a German soldier. Drawn in 1943, its importance lies in the shadowy figure, not with a gun or a dagger but with a pen, suggesting the resister gathering intelligence, the clandestine writer, poet, cartoonist, or journalist, the fabricator of false identity and ration cards, or the keeper of facts and statistics to record the crimes and inhumanities of the occupiers.

This was the dangerous, shadowy resistance action typified by Rose Valland at the Jeu de Paume art museum in Paris, where she memorized and kept details of the Nazi art thefts and spoliations, notably from Jewish collections, which were brought to the Jeu de Paume en route to Germany.

Her inside information was transmitted to resistance units who were able to prevent much of the art from reaching the frontier. None of her remarkable subversive activity over four years was rumbled by the Germans, who were at times suspicious of her but failed to realize that she understood German and listened in to their conversations and plans.

Her eventual memoir in 1961 was entitled *Le Front de l'art* (The Art Front) to indicate action at the front line. Another specific war.

Over fifty years later, in 2014, a film "based on a true story" of the recovery of stolen art was directed by George Clooney. Titled *The Monuments Men*, it was billed as a mix of history and comedy and featured the voluntarism of a group of military men distinctive for their individuality, and the secret resistance of a French museum curator, played by Cate Blanchett. It came at a time when the reality of individual resistance activity at all places of work, inside factories and mines, in the home, in the post offices, schools, museums, and doctors' surgeries, in the courts and, eventually, the police stations, was increasingly revealed, after years of piecemeal recognition, or neglect.

I don't need to emphasize just how gendered that neglect had been: the detailed history of women's diverse roles in resistance suffered badly. Excuses began to be made for this in the 1970s, but in the following half-century there was no excuse. George Clooney's movie still revelled in the military theater of collective male action and its mix of idealism and absurdity, but the route to a victorious outcome was found through the mass of secret information kept by the one main female character. It was an unacknowledged reference, but a reference nonetheless, to Rose Valland.

No one should underestimate how long it took to bring women's resistance from the margins of the story to where it is now, at the complex and heterogeneous center of resistance studies. This vital realignment was pioneered in the 1960s and 1970s in the face of ingrained gender prejudice, obstructive definitions of resistance, and the male acceptance of female self-effacement.

There is always a problem with self-effacement. To unpick it demands persistent questioning and deeper biographical research. It was a particular problem in the early testimonies after the war, but was still there even as late as the 1990s, for example in the testimony given to me by Simone Conquet in Cahors in March 1991, quoted at the end of Chapter 7. She was eventually offered the Médaille de la Résistance (Resistance medal) but said, "Give it to those who have suffered." And she added, "I wasn't a religious person . . . I wasn't a feminist really: it just seemed human decency to do something."

In similar ways many women have said the same thing, "It was just natural." "Natural"? "Ingrained"? "Instinctive"? Surely it was a choice.

The centrality of individual choice, agency, authorship, and subjectivity in history needs little extra emphasis today. Increasing numbers of individual women and men are now being named as actors in the resistance. This is not a way of making resistance less exceptional, but, rather, as the SOE agent Francis Cammaerts insisted, of asserting the exceptional and recognizing those ordinary people who should be known for their extraordinary achievements.

But as an interviewer you can all too easily miss the chance to find out more, due to the sheer force of an individual personality. I was in the border town of Annemasse, close to Switzerland, in 1969, interviewing a 73-year-old tailor, Jean Deffaugt, who had been appointed mayor of Annemasse by Vichy in 1943 but had links with resistance units in the area. Deffaugt wielded a heavy round black ruler which all tailors use, banging it on the table to convey the power of his story. He told me how, the year before, in 1968, he had been honored at Yad Vashem as one of the *Justes*, a "Righteous among the Nations" for having saved the lives of twenty-eight Jewish children aged from four to sixteen who had been caught by a German patrol on May 31, 1944, trying to reach Switzerland, shepherded by a young Jewish woman. They were interned in the Pax Hotel in Annemasse which the Gestapo had converted into a prison and torture chamber. Deffaugt had been informed by his resistance contacts and painfully negotiated a series of deals with the Gestapo commander in the town, finally offering him a safe conduct back to Germany at the liberation if he spared all the children. The commander agreed. The children were released in stages. All survived, and Jean Deffaugt kept his part of the bargain. The banging of the ruler increased dramatically as he told me of his fear and sleepless nights. He became very tired and asked for the recording to be stopped. I hoped to go back and redo the interview, but he died in the following year before that could happen. I had great regrets.

Later my even greater regret was that I had not pressed him to tell me what he knew about the woman who was shepherding the children by stealth toward the frontier. I had found out that her name was Marianne Cohn. She was born in Mannheim, to German-Jewish intellectuals who took refuge in France but were sent to the horrendous Vichy internment camp at Gurs in the southwest. Marianne herself found a way of surviving and a new purpose in the Jewish scout movement which was surprisingly permitted to exist by Vichy for two years until 1942.[5] From there she went underground as an active resister, seeking safety for Jewish children by finding them hiding places or securing their safe passage out of the country. Imprisoned with the children in Annemasse, she refused a plan to be rescued while any of the children was still being held. She was tortured but gave nothing away. "I have saved 200 children," she said to the Gestapo, adding, "I will continue to save more." On July 8, 1944, a Gestapo murder squad from Lyon which included members of the notorious Vichy Milice took her and five others from the Annemasse prison and kicked and hacked them to death in a nearby wood, using their boots and heavy metal spades. She was twenty-one. Two months later Annemasse was liberated. Only in the 1980s did I find out these facts of her life, and then I understood the determination behind the poem she had written during an earlier period of imprisonment in Nice: "Je trahirai demain, pas aujourd'hui" ("I will betray tomorrow, not today"). It became her recurrent words of choice and defiance, "Not today."

The range of sources, material, and techniques now used in the current rediscovery and reevaluation of resistance lives is exemplary. Insights from anthropology, family history, gender studies, life-history research, oral history, film, and fiction have made this one of the most exciting areas of contemporary history in its best interdisciplinary mode.

The focus on deception and bluff is one of the key areas. The soutane of priests and the habits of nuns were used as cover. So, too, were the shopping bag, the school satchel, the pram, the goods of travelling salesmen, the uniforms of nurse and social worker, the bags of doctors, medical students, and midwives, the pretense of pregnancy, the ploy of appearing stupid, the whistling of the Vichy anthem to Pétain, the overt reading of the Nazi magazine *Signal*, the gregarious chatter of the "woman at the doorway," keeping the police or Gestapo waiting while documents were hidden and people had time to escape.

There is renewed interest in Lucie Aubrac's 1984 memoir which includes the story of her epic resistance charade as a wronged aristocratic mistress, elaborately played out to rescue her husband Raymond. Her account is well translated as "Outwitting the Gestapo." Once transported to safety in London, they made instant journalistic copy, with Lucie as the heroine of a strip cartoon.

The whole approach to personalities, the assumption of code names and new identities, and lives reshaped in resistance activity has been brilliantly stimulated by Juliette Pattinson's study of the training of men and women of the British SOE about to be dropped into France. Her book, largely based on oral testimony, is titled *Behind Enemy Lines: Gender, Passing and the Special Operations Executive in the Second World War*. Her chapter subheadings show the originality of her approach: "Taught how to play a part"; "Living a different life: performing heroic and stoic masculinities"; "The best disguise: performing femininities for clandestine purposes." It could be labelled a theater of dissimulation.

Because of the originality of so much resistance activity, historians have faced the need to be almost as creative as resistance itself. In Juliette Pattinson's work, the two are brought together: the ingenuity of resistance at the time, and the ingenuity of historical theory and insight.

The woman with a pistol on the cover of her book is Jaqueline Nearne from the 1947 documentary film on the workings of SOE, *School for Danger*, later released in a longer version as *Now It Can be Told*. Featuring two of SOE's outstanding agents, Harry Rée and Jacqueline Nearne herself, the film is now being rediscovered and widely used.[6]

Partly shot in late 1944 in liberated parts of the French south, the film depicts training, and action in the field, revealed for the first time as a historical record. It has now become an essential reference point for the study of postwar representations of resistance activity, whether in film, video, or audiotape, along with the French film on railway resistance, *La bataille du rail* (The Battle of the Rails) made in 1946 by René Clément, with substantial roles played by ex-resistance railway workers.

The contrivances of these two very early postwar films are many, while the upbeat, positive verve of both has provoked every reaction, from strong emotional identification to varying degrees of skepticism.

We have to weave both these films into the very story that can, and should, be told. Audiences have been most attracted by video and film details of people and places which show resistance action in its most observable form: sabotage, rescue, escape, piloting planes by the light of the moon, parachuting at night, small camouflaged fishing boats navigated in the dark in and out of the coves of Brittany and the Mediterranean. In these actions the difference between traditional warfare and resistance activity can easily be grasped. And gender stereotypes are repeatedly blurred. Only recently the obituaries about the ninety-year-old Sonia d'Artois, dropped into France in 1944 by the SOE, and active in the guerrilla warfare of maquis units in the area of Le Mans, have reminded us that she was sent over not only as a liaison agent but also as an arms and explosives expert, to instruct sabotage groups in ways to blow up railway lines and German supply depots.

Sabotage had its detractors at the time. Secret state-run intelligence services were, and still are, critical. The consequences of sabotage could not be controlled, they maintain, whereas for many resisters, sabotage was an ontological proof of existence, a sign of pragmatic commitment; the "something," however small, that could be done, the active move from refusal to revolt. As such, the derailing of a train features in almost any film on resistance as a necessity: it is there in 1947 in *Now It Can Be Told* and fifty years later it is at the start of the film *Lucie Aubrac,* directed by Claude Berri, discussed in Chapter 3.

Harry Rée of SOE liked to have the last word on this issue. One of the central aims of his resistance initiatives was to minimize deaths, something that sabotage could do, but aerial bombing could not.[7]

If derailment of a train is the filmic logo, or signature, of resistance activity, stories and documentaries of rescue and escape are the heart of its ethical history. American opinion, for example, quick to be critical of contemporary France, warmed to French resistance through the highly effective and affective documentary made by Pierre Sauvage in 1989. Titled *Les Armes de l'esprit* (Weapons of the Spirit), it brought into the public domain the shelter and rescue of hundreds of Jewish children in Le Chambon-sur-Lignon, a remote Protestant village on the Vivarais-Lignon plateau in the southeast of the Massif Central. It was the plateau where Sauvage was born and where he and his Jewish parents survived. There is continued criticism that the film concentrates too narrowly on the pacifist motivation of certain Protestant pastors and exaggerates the number of children saved, but critics do not seek to deny the emotional strength of the film and its recorded testimonies.

Had Michelin issued guides and maps to resistance as it did for the battlefields of World War 1, they would have taken us to Le Chambon-sur-Lignon as to countless other places where secret hideouts and rescue lines, for downed Allied aircrew, resisters on the run, or Jewish children, defined the local resistance. In pursuit of place, they might even have been attracted to the house in the Sussex village of Bignor, mentioned in the last chapter, used as a secret staging post for resistance agents en route to or from France via the airfield of Tangmere near Chichester. It probably seems an excess of bathos to mention Bignor after the plateau of Vivarais-Lignon, but the multifarious stories of resistance inside and outside France are an entry point into a transnational understanding of *L'armée des ombres*.

Conscious that history has a public function, and, potentially, an impact on government policy formation at all levels, I believe this is a prescient moment in time for historians to register Resistance as a genre of historical activity, comparable to revolution and war, both of which for decades have had their centers of study and their archives in almost all cultures and nations.

Responding to this challenge, new museums of resistance in France, and rejuvenated regional archives, have diversified Nora's national *lieux de mémoire* and have found new truths and new sites of memory in a multiform national history. Foreigners, ethnic minorities, refugees, and immigrant workers are now included and named in the diffuse story of resistance action, particularly at the local level. Still more, individual memories, sidelined by Nora's emphasis on collective memory, are now prominent. The generic study of Resistance in history is bringing resisters out of the shadows.

The pioneering Archive of Resistance Testimony at the University of Sussex, directed by Chris Warne within a Center of Resistance Studies, is an ambitious initiative, starting with testimony to all aspects of resistance in France in the Second World War, and moving outward, forward, and backward, to the anti-Apartheid struggle in South Africa, the anti-Stalinist resistance in Eastern Europe, the civil rights movements in the United States and elsewhere, colonial resistance, the resistance of pacifists to war and of slaves to slavery, and the struggles of indigenous peoples.

Closely linked to these initiatives, and an active symptom of community interest in Resistance history, there is the Secret WW2 Learning Network, already mentioned, which specializes in "the covert Allied operations during the Second World War with a focus on those who took part in clandestine operations in support of resistance in occupied France."[8]

Given this width of actual and potential testimony, there is a necessity to have ongoing debates about definitions and criteria of Resistance.

First, the fight for freedom and justice, NOT the fight for a rival oppressive absolutism, must surely be a fundamental criterion of Resistance across time and place.

Second, the voluntary commitment of civilians to the subterfuge, creativity, secrecy, and subversion necessary to fight against overwhelming and unacceptable oppression must also be fundamental.

And third, I would add, the aim is to establish, restore, or extend human rights.

The wide-angled lens of resistance studies will always have peaceful protest at one end and war at the other. Somewhere between the two lie both active resistance and revolution. They are not interchangeable, but they are often inextricable. In the eighteenth century, the resistance of slaves themselves to their inhuman enslavement in the Caribbean provided a model of prolonged protest, revolt, and subversion immediately before and notably after the French Revolution, but when led by the black General Toussaint Louverture in the French colony of Saint Domingue which later became Haiti, the resistance and liberation of slaves were inextricably caught up in revolution and war. Nevertheless, his plaque in the Paris Panthéon emphasizes his life as a resister: *Combattant de la liberté, artisan de l'abolition de l'esclavage* (Fighter for liberty, artisan of the abolition of slavery).

In the twentieth century, resistance to apartheid in South Africa, and the civil rights movement in the United States in the 1960s, are perhaps the clearest examples of cultural, political, and civilian resistance without war or revolution, where the fight for human freedom, rights, and justice was all-consuming.

Whatever the disillusionments that have followed, and whatever still needs to be done, the liberation from apartheid and racial segregation like the liberation from Nazism, like the end of Stalinist tyranny over Russia and Eastern Europe, like the freedoms gained by colonized peoples were moments to register the role played over years by resistance.

Peaceful, nonviolent resistance, associated for most people with Gandhi and Martin Luther King, is rightly explored and admired as one major type of resistance in Howard Caygill's wide-ranging and perceptive study, titled *On Resistance: a Philosophy of Defiance*. In the *Guardian* review of the book, Jacqueline Rose summed up Gandhi's practice: "Such resistance is sustained not by violence but by legitimacy that in turn creates a kind of freedom." Yes, indeed.

And there is also just such a freedom created by legitimacy together with a readiness for armed conflict, and that is the story to be told of French Resistance. It falls within and outside military history. It highlights civilian history at the grass roots. We need to argue about its rationale, to continue to bring the history of the *armée des ombres* out of the footnotes, and to remember its achievements and its mistakes, its dead, its deported, its defiance of torture. The research is there to be pursued more widely; local novels, videography, the audio interview, and the archival document are voices that need to be heard at all levels of education and in all communities. I turn again to Stéphane Hessel, French resister, concentration camp survivor, and one of the architects of the UN Declaration of Human Rights, who died in 2014. He always liked to end his testimony with the words, "To those who will make the 21st Century I affectionately say 'Créer c'est Résister, Résister c'est Créer'" ("To create is to resist. To resist is to create"). It is not a bad ending. It is an even better beginning.

Notes

Chapter 1

1 Françoise Meifredy (with the collaboration of Robert Hervet), *Missions sans frontières* (Paris, France-Empire, 1966), 18–31.

2 Paul Simon, *One Enemy Only–the Invader*, preface by General de Gaulle, trans. W. G. Corp (London: Hodder & Stoughton, 1942), 5.

3 Sébastien Albertelli, "Une Résistance londonienne?" in Julien Blanc and Cécile Vast (eds.), *Chercheurs en Résistance* (Rennes: Presses Universitaires de Rennes, 2014), 34.

4 H. R. Kedward, *In Search of the Maquis: Rural Resistance in Southern France, 1942–1944* (Oxford: Oxford University Press, 1993), 275–9.

5 Stéphane Hessel, *Indignez-vous!* (Montpellier: Indigène éditions, 2010).

6 H. R. Kedward, *Resistance in Vichy France: A Study of Ideas and Motivation in the Southern Zone 1940–1942* (Oxford: Oxford University Press, 1978), 256–9.

7 Ibid., 250–3.

8 Kedward, *In Search of the Maquis*, 236–9. Henri Cordesse, *La Libération en Lozère, 1944–1945* (Cordesse: n.p., 1977).

Chapter 2

1 Henry Rousso, *Le Syndrome de Vichy, 1944–198 . . .* (Paris: Seuil, 1987).

2 M. R. D. Foot, *SOE in France* (London: HMSO, 1966), 50.

3 André Roure, *Valeur de la Vie Humaine* (Paris: Sfelt, 1947).

4 Cited in Pierre Bolle, ed., *Le Plateau Vivarais-Lignon: Accueil et Résistance 1939–1944* (Le Chambon-sur-Lignon: Société d'Histoire de la Montagne, 1992), 69.

5 James C. Scott, *Weapons of the Weak: Everyday Forms of Peasant Resistance* (Newhaven and London: Yale University Press, 1985).

6 *No Ordinary People* directed by Mike Fox for Foxy Films, shown on BBC 2 on November 28, 1995.

7 Kedward, *In Search of the Maquis*, 244–5.

Chapter 3

1 See Pascal Convert, *Raymond Aubrac, Résister, reconstruire, transmettre* (Paris: Seuil, 2011), 646–56.

2 David Lan, *Guns and Rain: Guerillas and Spirit Mediums in Zimbabwe* (Berkeley and Los Angeles: James Currey and University of California Press, 1985).

Chapter 4

1 Alexander Werth, *The Last Days of Paris* (London: Hamish Hamilton, 1940), 213.

2 *French Writing on English Soil*, selected and trans. J. G. Weightman (London: Sylvan Press, 1945), 7.

3 Michel Goubet et Paul Debauges, *Histoire de la Résistance dans la Haute-Garonne* (Toulouse: Editions Milan, 1986), 10–11.

4 François Bédarida described it as "un sursaut de conscience" in his essay, "Sur le concept de Résistance," in Jean-Marie Guillon and Pierre Laborie (eds.), *Mémoire et Histoire: la Résistance* (Toulouse: Privat, 1995), 49.

5 See Armelle Mabon, *Prisonniers de Guerre 'indigènes': Visages oubliés de la France occupée* (Paris: La Découverte, 2010), 115–33, and Nancy Wood, *Germaine Tillion, une femme-mémoire* (Paris: Autrement, 2003), 52–70. See also the documentary *Oubliés et Trahis* listed in the Bibliography under Film titles.

6 Donald Caskie, *The Tartan Pimpernel* (London: Oldbourne, 1957), 36.

7 *Varian Fry, du refuge . . .* (Arles: Actes Sud, 2000), 8, 68, and 26. The papers are published in two volumes, edited by Jean-Marie Guillon, the first *Varian Fry du refuge . . .* and the second *Varian Fry . . . à l'exil*. See also, Daniel Bénédite, *La filière marseillaise: Un Chemin vers la liberté sous l'occupation* (Paris: Clancier Guénaud, 1984).

8 Adam Rayski, "Réflexion sur l'historiographie de la résistance juive," in Serge Wolikow (dir), *Les Images Collectives de la Résistance* (Dijon: EUD, 1997), 39.

9 *Varian Fry, du refuge . . .*, 73.

10 Kedward, *In Search of the Maquis*, 234.

11 Tzvetan Todorov, *L'Homme dépaysé* (Seuil, 1996), 22–3.

12 J. G. Weightman, ed. and trans., *French Writing on English Soil* (London: Sylvan Press), 22–3.

13 Gérard Noiriel, *Les origines républicaines de Vichy* (Paris: Hachette, 1999), 276–9; Karen Adler's doctorate was titled "Idealizing France, 1942–1948: The Place of Gender and Race," University of Sussex, 1998. Her published title

is *Jews and Gender in Liberation France* (Cambridge: Cambridge University Press, 2003).

14 Noiriel, *Les origines républicaines de Vichy*, 279.

15 Kedward, *In Search of the Maquis*, 233–5.

Chapter 5

1 See the volume of essays in honor of Douglas Johnson: Martyn Cornick and Ceri Crossley, eds., *Problems in French History* (London: Palgrave, 2000).

2 Author's interview with Lucie Aubrac, broadcast by BBC Radio 4 in the program, "De Gaulle and French Resistance," June 24, 1980.

3 Georges Guingouin, *Quatre ans de lutte sur le sol limousin* (Paris: Hachette, 1974), 9.

4 François Marcot, ed., *Dictionnaire historique de la Résistance* (Paris: Robert Laffont, 2006), 437. De Gaulle's words quoted in Michel Taubmann, *L'Affaire Guingouin* (Limoges: Lucien Souny, 1994), 29: I am grateful to Peter Holmes for first bringing this book to my attention.

5 Guingouin, *Quatre ans de lutte sur*, 22.

6 Archives nationales, Fic III 1197, Haute-Vienne, Prefect's reports, April 6 and June 4, 1943.

7 Jacques Revel, "La Nation," in Pierre Nora (ed.), *Les Lieux de mémoire: Les France* (Paris: Gallimard, 1992), 850.

8 Louis Le Moigne and Marcel Barbanceys, *L'Armée Secrète en Haute-Corrèze, 1942–44* (Moulins: Association des amicales des maquis AS de Haute Corrèze, 1979), 10.

9 Jean-Laurent Voneau, *Le Procès de Bordeaux: les Malgré-Nous et le drame d'Oradour* (Strasbourg: Editions du Rhin, 2003), 400.

10 Douglas Johnson, *France and the World Beyond* (London: UCL, 1970), 8.

11 Quoted by Taubmann, *L'Affaire Guingouin*, 308.

12 Vincent Brousse, Dominique Danthieux and Philippe Grandcoing, *1905 le printemps rouge de Limoges, Culture et Patrimoine en Limousin* (Limoges: Pulim, 2005), 115.

13 François Boulet, "Deux montagnes-maquis exemplaires dans la France occupée (1943–1944): la montagne limousine et la Haute-Savoie," in Vincent Brousse and Philippe Grandcoing (eds.), *Un Siècle militant, engagement(s), résistance(s) et mémoire(s) au XXe Siècle en Limousin* (Limoges: Pulim, 2005), 35–84.

14 Les Amis du Musée de la Résistance du Département de la Haute-Vienne, *Bulletin*, 57 (2002): 7.

15 Kedward, *In Search of the Maquis*, 244–5.

Chapter 6

1 Quoted by Steven Poole in his obituary of Jean Baudrillard in *The Guardian*, March 8, 2007, 39.

2 Published by La Découverte, 2007.

3 Published by Denoël, 2004, and awarded the Prix Renaudot, the first time that the prize was awarded posthumously.

4 *Suite française*, 402, 407.

5 *La Vie d'Irène Némirovsky, 1903–1942* (Paris: Grasset, Denoël), 2007.

6 Susan Sontag, "Pay Attention to the World," in *The Guardian*, March 17, 2007, Review section, 4–6.

7 Daniel Aaron, *American Notes: Selected Essays* (Lebanon, New Hampshire: Northeastern University Press, 1994), 232.

8 Published by Gallimard, 2006, it was awarded the Prix Goncourt.

9 See, in particular, Luc Capdevila, *Les Bretons au lendemain de l'Occupation: Imaginaire et comportement d'une sortie de guerre 1944–1945* (Rennes: Presses Universitaires de Rennes, 1999).

10 Jacques Chardonne, *Chronique privée de l'an 1940* (Paris: Stock, 1941), 118. Quoted in Philippe Burrin, *La France à l'heure allemande, 1940–1944* (Paris: Seuil, 1995), 409.

11 Germaine Tillion, *Le Verfügbar aux Enfers: Une opérette à Ravensbrück* (Paris: Editions de la Martinière, 2005). Wood, *Germaine Tillion, une femme-mémoire: D'une Algérie à l'autre.*

12 Paul Virilio, *Ville Panique* (Paris: Galilée, 2004).

13 Paul La Farge, writing in *Nextbook, a new read on Jewish culture*, posted on the web on December 9, 2006, criticized her for "a wilful blindness" toward the possibilities, and justifications, of resistance.

Chapter 7

1 Robert Frank, "Angleterre," in François Marcot (ed.), *Dictionnaire Historique de la Résistance* (Paris: Robert Laffont, 2006), 322–5.

2 Barbara Bertram, *French Resistance in Sussex* (Pulborough: Barnworks Publishing, 1995).

3 Paul McCue, *Brighton's Secret Agents* (London: Uniform Publishing Group, 2016). See also: https://www.secret-war2.net/; David Howarth, *The Shetland Bus* (1951), and later editions.

4 Jean-Louis Crémieux-Brilhac, ed. *Les Voix de la Liberté: Ici Londres 1940–1944*, Vol. 1 (Paris: La Documentation Française, 1975), xxvi.

5 *Maquis en Gâtinais* (AHVOL, 1994); Anne Thoraval, *Paris: Les Lieux de la Résistance* (Paris: Parigramme, 2007).

6 Agnès Humbert, *Résistance. Memoirs of Occupied France*, trans. with notes, Barbara Mellor; Afterword by Julien Blanc (London: Bloomsbury, 2008).

7 Matthew Cobb, *Eleven Days in August: The Liberation of Paris in 1944* (London: Simon & Schuster, 2013), 366.

8 Ibid., 208.

9 Jean Guéhenno, *Journal des Années Noires* (Paris: Gallimard, 1947), 505.

10 Hélène Berr, *Journal 1942–1944* (Paris: Tallandier, 2008), 282 and *passim*.

11 Kedward, *In Search of the Maquis*, 263–4. For Jean-Jacques Chapou, see Georges Cazard, *Capitaine Philippe, ou l'histoire du Lot au travers de la biographie de J. J. Chapou* (Cahors: Imprimerie Coueslant, 1950).

12 Kedward, *In Search of the Maquis*, 278.

13 Jonathan Rée, ed, *A Schoolmaster's War: Harry Rée, British Agent in the French Resistance* (New Haven and London: Yale University Press, 2020).

14 Kedward, *Resistance in Vichy France*, 273–6.

Chapter 8

1 Jean-Louis Crémieux-Brilhac, *La France Libre: de l'Appel du 18 juin à la Libération* (Paris: Gallimard, 1996), 278. See Debra Kelly, "Mapping Free French London: Places, Spaces, Traces," in Debra Kelly and Martyn Cornick (eds.), *A History of the French in London: Liberty, Equality, Opportunity* (London: Institute of Historical Research, 2013), 340–1.

2 Kedward, *In Search of the Maquis*, 242.

3 Paul Silvestre, "STO, maquis et guerrilla dans l'Isère," *Revue d'Histoire de la Deuxième Guerre Mondiale*, 130 (1983): 16–17.

4 Jacques Debû-Bridel, *Les Editions de Minuit: Historique et Bibliographie* (Paris: Editions de Minuit, 1945), 10.

5 See Daniel Lee, *Pétain's Jewish Children: French Jewish Youth and the Vichy Regime, 1940–1942* (Oxford: Oxford U.P., 2014).

6 Imperial War Museum, *Now It Can Be Told*, 2007.

7 See Rée, ed., *A Schoolmaster's War*.

8 See : https://www.secret-war2.net/

Bibliography

Introductory Note

For the widest number of entries and essays on all aspects of resistance in France, and the most comprehensive bibliography, see the *Dictionnaire Historique de la Résistance*, edited by François Marcot in collaboration with Bruno Leroux and Christine Levisse-Touzé, Paris, Robert Laffont, 2006.
It is indispensable, not least for its culminating sections headed "Anthropologie de la vie résistante" and "Mémoires de la résistance" which include the important role played by poetry, and titles of significant films on the resistance.(See later, **Bibliography 2** and **3**)

1. HISTORY, BIOGRAPHY, MEMORIES, INTERPRETATIONS

Adler, Jacques, *The Jews of Paris and the Final Solution: Communal Response and Internal Conflicts, 1940–1944*, New York and Oxford: Oxford University Press, 1987.

Adler, K.H., *Jews and Gender in Liberation France*, Cambridge: Cambridge University Press, 2003.

Aglan, Alya, *Mémoires résistantes, le réseau Jade-Fitzroy (1940–1944)*, Paris: Le Cerf, 1994.

Aglan, Alya, *La Résistance sacrifiée: Le movement "Libération-Nord" (1940–1947)*, Paris: Flammarion, 1999.

Aglan, Alya, *Le Temps de la Résistance*, Arles: Actes Sud, 2008.

Aglan, Alya, *La France à l'envers: La guerre de Vichy (1940–1945)*, Paris: Gallimard, 2020.

Aglan, Alya and Jean-Pierre Azéma, eds., *Jean Cavaillès Résistant ou la Pensée en actes*, Paris: Flammarion, 2002.

Ajchenbaum, Yves-Marc, *A la Vie A la Mort: Histoire du journal Combat 1941–1974*, Paris: Le Monde Éditions, 1994.

Albertelli, Sébastien, *Les Services Secrets du Général de Gaulle: Le BCRA, 1940–1944*, Paris: Perrin, 2009.

Albertelli, Sébastien, Julien Blanc, and Laurent Douzou, *La Lutte Clandestine en France, Une histoire de la Résistance en France 1940–1944*, Paris: Seuil, 2019.

Andrieu, Claire, *Le Programme commun de la Résistance: Des idées dans la guerre*, Paris: Éditions de l'Érudit, 1984.

Andrieu, Claire, *Tombés du Ciel: Le sort des pilotes abattus en Europe 1939–1945*, Paris: Tallandier, 2021.

d'Aragon, Charles, *La Résistance sans Héroisme*, intro. by Guillaume Piketty, Geneva: Éditions du Tricorne, 2001.

Ashdown, Paddy, *The Cruel Victory: The French Resistance, D-Day and the Battle for the Vercors 1944*, London: William Collins, 2014.

d'Astier de la Vigerie, Emmanuel, *Sept fois sept jours*, Paris: Éditions de Minuit, 1947.

Aubrac, Lucie, *Ils partiront dans l'ivresse*, Paris: Seuil, 1984. Translated by Konrad Bieber as *Outwitting the Gestapo*, Lincoln: University of Nebraska Press, 1993.

Aubrac, Raymond, *Où la mémoire s'attarde*, Paris: Odile Jacob, 1996.

Aubrac, Raymond and Renaud Helfer-Aubrac, *Passage de témoin*, Paris: Calmann-Lévy, 2011.

Azéma, Jean-Pierre, *De Munich à la Libération 1938–1944*, Paris: Seuil, 1979. Translated by Janet Lloyd as *From Munich to the Liberation 1938–1944*, Cambridge: Cambridge University Press, and Paris: Éditions de la Maison des Sciences de l'Homme, 1984.

Azéma, Jean-Pierre, *Jean Moulin, le politique, le rebelle, le résistant*, Paris: Perrin, 2003.

Azéma, Jean-Pierre and François Bédarida, *La France des années noires*, 2 vols., Paris: Seuil, 1993.

Azéma, Jean-Pierre, François Bédarida, and Daniel Cordier, *Jean Moulin et l.e Conseil national de la Résistance*, Paris: CNRS, 1983.

Azéma, Jean-Pierre, François Bédarida, and Robert Frank, eds., *Jean Moulin et la Résistance en 1943*, Paris: Cahiers de l'IHTP No.27, June 1994.

Bailey, Roderick, in association with the Imperial War Museum, *Forgotten Voices of the Secret War: An Inside History of Special Operations during the Second World War*, London: Ebury Press, 2008.

Baudoin, Madeleine, *Histoire des groupes francs (M. U. R.) des Bouches-du-Rhône de septembre 1943 à la libération*, Paris: P.U.F., 1962.

Bédarida, François, ed., *Normandie 44: Du Débarquement à la libération*, Paris: Albin Michel, 1987.

Bédarida, François and Jean-Pierre Azéma, eds., *La France des Années Noires*, Paris: Seuil, 1993.

Bédarida, Renée, *Les Armes de l'Esprit, "Témoignage chrétien": 1941–1944*, Paris: Éditions ouvrières, 1977.

Bédarida, Renée and François Bédarida, *La Résistance spirituelle, 1941–1944: les cahiers clandestins du "Témoignage chrétien,"* Paris: Alban Michel, 2001.

Bellanger, Claude, *La Presse Clandestine, 1940–1944*, Paris: Armand Colin, 1961.

Berr, Hélène, *Journal*, Paris: Tallandier, 2008.

Bertram, Barbara, *French Resistance in Sussex*, Pulborough: Barnworks, 1995.

Blanc, Julien, *Au commencement de la Résistance: Du côté du musée de l'Homme 1940–1941*, Paris: Seuil, 2010.

Blanc, Julien and Cécile Vast, eds., *Chercheurs en Résistance: Pistes et outils à l'usage des historiens*, Rennes: Presses Universitaires de Rennes, 2014.

Bolle, Pierre, ed., *Grenoble et le Vercors: De la Résistance à la Libération*, Grenoble: Presses Universitaires de Grenoble, 2003.

Bolle, Pierre, ed., *Le Plateau Vivarais-Lignon: Accueil et Résistance 1939–1944*, Le Chambon-sur-Lignon: Société d'histoire de la Montagne, 1992.

Bourderon, Roger, *Libération du Languedoc méditerranéen*, Paris: Hachette, 1974.

Bourderon, Roger, *Rol-Tanguy*, Paris: Tallandier, 2004.

Bourderon, Roger, *Le PCF à l'épreuve de la guerre, 1940–1943: de la guerre impérialiste à la lutte armée*, Paris: Éditions Syllepse, 2012.

Bourdet, Claude, *L'Aventure incertaine*, Paris: Stock, 1975.

Broch, Ludivine, *Ordinary Workers, Vichy and the Holocaust: French Railwaymen and the Second World War*, Cambridge: Cambridge University Press, 2016.

Brossat, Alain, *Les Tondues: un carnaval moche*, Paris: Manya, 1992.

Canaud, Jacques, *Les Maquis du Morvan 1943–1944*, Château-Chinon: Académie du Morvan, 1981.

Capdevila, Luc, *Les Bretons au lendemain de l'occupation: Imaginaire et comportement d'une sortie de guerre (1944–1945)*, Rennes: Presses Universitaires de Rennes, 1999.

Capdevila, Luc, François Rouquet, Fabrice Virgili, and Danièle Voldman, *Hommes et Femmes dans la France en Guerre (1914–1945)*, Paris: Payot, 2003.

Cappelletto, Francesca, ed., *Memory and World War II: An Ethnographical Approach*, which includes Riki Van Boeschoten, "'Little Moscow' and the Greek Civil War," Oxford and New York: Berg, 2005.

Caskie, Donald, *The Tartan Pimpernel*, London: Oldbourne, 1957.

Cassou, Jean, *La Mémoire courte*, Paris: Éditions de Minuit, 1953.

Catalogue des Périodiques Clandestins diffusés en France de 1939 à 1944, Paris: Bibliothèque Nationale, 1954.

Caygill, Howard, *On Resistance: A Philosophy of Defiance*, London: Bloomsbury, 2013.

Cazard, Georges, en collaboration avec Marcel Metges, *Capitaine Philippe, ou l'histoire du maquis du Lot au travers de la biographie de J. J. Chapou*, Cahors: Imprimerie Coueslant, 1950, 2nd ed., 1984.

Chatel, Nicole, ed., *Des Femmes dans la Résistance*, Paris: Julliard, 1972.

CLIO, Histoire, Femmes et Société: No.1, Résistances et Libérations (France 1940–1945), Toulouse: Presses Universitaires du Mirail, 1995.

Closon, Francis-Louis, *Le Temps des passions*, Paris: Presses de la Cité, 1974.

Cobb, Matthew, *The Resistance: The French Fight Against the Nazis*, London: Simon & Schuster, 2009.

Cobb, Matthew, *Eleven Days in August: The Liberation of Paris in 1944*, London: Simon & Schuster, 2013.

Cointet, Michèle and Jean-Paul Cointet, eds., *Dictionnaire historique de la France sous l'Occupation*, Paris: Tallandier, 2000.

Comte, Bernard, *L'honneur et la conscience: Catholiques français en résistance (1940–1944)*, Paris: Les Éditions de l'Atelier, 1998.

Conan, Éric and Henry Rousso, *Vichy, un passé qui ne passe pas*, Paris: Gallimard, 1994.

Convert, Pascal, *Raymond Aubrac, Résister, Reconstruire, Transmettre*, Paris: Seuil, 2011.

Conway, Martin and José Gotovitch, eds., *Europe in Exile: European Exile Communities in Britain 1940–45*, New York and Oxford: Berghahn, 2001.

Cordier, Daniel, *Jean Moulin, l'inconnu du Panthéon*, 3 vols., Paris: Jean-Claude Lattès, 1989–1993.

Cordier, Daniel, *Jean Moulin: La République des Catacombes*, Paris: Gallimard, 1999.

Cordier, Daniel, *Alias Caracalla: Mémoires 1940–1943*, Paris: Gallimard, 2009.

Courtois, Stéphane, *Le PCF dans la guerre: de Gaulle, la Résistance, Staline*, Paris: Ramsay, 1980.

Courtois, Stéphane, Denis Peschanski, and Adam Rayski, *Le Sang de l'étranger: Les immigrés de la MOI dans la Résistance*, Paris: Fayard, 1989.

Crémieux-Brilhac, Jean-Louis, ed., *Les Voix de la Liberté: Ici Londres, 1940–1944*, 5 vols., Paris: La Documentation Française, 1975.

Crémieux- Brilhac, Jean-Louis, *La France Libre: de l'appel du 18 juin à la Libération*, Paris: Gallimard, 1996.

Diamant, David, *Les Juifs dans la Résistance française 1940–1944*, Paris: Roger Maria, 1971.

Diamond, Hanna, *Women and the Second World War in France, 1939–48, Choices and Constraints*, New York: Longman/Pearson Education Ltd, 1999.

Diamond, Hanna, *Fleeing Hitler: France 1940*, Oxford: Oxford University Press, 2007.

Diamond, Hanna and Simon Kitson, eds., *Vichy, Resistance, Liberation: New Perspectives on Wartime France*, Oxford and New York: Berg, 2005.

Douzou, Laurent, *La Désobéissance, histoire d'un mouvement et d'un journal clandestins: Libération-Sud (1940–1944)*, Paris: Odile Jacob, 1995.

Douzou, Laurent, *La Résistance française: une histoire périlleuse*, Paris: Seuil, 2005.

Douzou, Laurent, *Lucie Aubrac*, Paris: Perrin, 2009.

Douzou, Laurent, ed., *Faire l'histoire de la Résistance*, Rennes: Presses Universitaires de Rennes, 2010.

Douzou, Laurent, Robert Frank, Denis Peschanski, and Dominique Veillon, eds., *La Résistance et l.es Français: Villes, centres et logiques de décision*, Cachan: Actes du Colloque international, IHTP, 1995.

Drake, David, *Paris at War, 1939–1944*, Cambridge, MA: Harvard University Press, 2015.

Dunstan, Sarah, *Race, Rights and Reform: Black Activism in the French Empire and the United States from World War 1 to the Cold War*, Cambridge: Cambridge University Press, 2021.

Evans, Martin, *The Memory of Resistance: French Opposition to the Algerian War (1954–1962)*, Oxford and New York: Berg, 1997.

Farmer, Sarah, *Martyred Village: Commemorating the 1944 Massacre at Oradour-sur-Glane*, Berkeley and Los Angeles: University of California Press, 1999.

Fayol, Pierre, *Le Chambon-sur-Lignon sous l'Occupation (1940–1944), Les résistances locales, l'aide interalliée, l'action de Virginia Hall (O. S. S.)*, Paris: L'Harmattan, 1990.

Fishman, Sarah, *We Will Wait: Wives of French Prisoners of War, 1940–1945*, New Haven and London: Yale University Press, 1991.

Fishman, Sarah, Laura Lee Downs, Ioannis Sinanoglou, Leonard V. Smith, and Robert Zaretsky, eds., *France at War. Vichy and the Historians*, Oxford and New York: Berg, 2000.

Foot, M. R. D., *SOE in France*, London: HMSO, 1966. New edition, London: Frank Cass, 2004.

Foot, M. R. D., *Resistance*, London: Eyre Methuen, 1976. New edition with added subtitle, *European Resistance to the Nazis, 1940–1945*, London: Biteback, 2016.

Foot, M. R. D., *Six Faces of Courage: Secret Agents Against Nazi Tyranny*, London: Eyre Methuen, 1978. Revised and updated edition, Barnsley: Leo Cooper, 2003.

Footitt, Hilary, *War and Liberation in France: Living with the Liberators*, London: Palgrave, 2004.

Footitt, Hilary and John Simmonds, *France 1943–1945*, Leicester: Leicester University Press, 1988.

Fourcade, Marie-Madeleine, *L'Arche de Noé*, Paris: Fayard, 1968.

Frank, Robert and José Gotovitch, eds., *La Résistance et les Européens du Nord*, Brussels: CEGES, 1994.

Frenay, Henri, *La nuit finira: Mémoires de Résistance, 1940–1945*, Paris: Robert Laffont, 1973.

Funk, Arthur, *Hidden Ally: The French Resistance, Special Operations and the Landings in Southern France, 1944*, New York: Greenwood Press, 1992.

Gabert, Michèle, *Entrés en Résistance: Isère, Des hommes et des femmes dans la Résistance*, Grenoble: Presses Universitaires de Grenoble, 2000.

de Gaulle, Charles, *Mémoires de Guerre*, 3 vols, Paris: Plon, 1954–1959.

de Gaulle, Geneviève, *La Traversée de la nuit*, Paris: Seuil, 1998.

Gex le Verrier, Madeleine, *Une Française dans la tourmente*, London: Hamish Hamilton, 1942. New edition, edited by Julien Blanc, Paris: Éditions du Félin, 2020.

Gildea, Robert, *Fighters in the Shadows: A New History of the French Resistance*, London: Faber & Faber, 2015.

Gilzmer, Mechtild, Christine Levisse-Touzé, and Stefan Martens, eds., *Les Femmes dans la Résistance en France*, Paris: Tallandier, 2003.

Gorrara, Claire, *Women's Representations of the Occupation in post-'68 France*, London: Macmillan and New York: St. Martin's Press, 1998.

Granet, Marie, *Ceux de la Résistance, 1940–1944*, Paris: Éditions de Minuit, 1964.

Guéhenno, Jean, *Journal des années noires (1940–1944)*, Paris: Gallimard, 1947.

Guillon, Jean-Marie, *La Résistance dans le Var: Essai d'histoire politique*, Thèse de l'université d'Aix-Marseille I, 1989.

Guillon, Jean-Marie, ed., *Varian Fry du refuge . . . à l'exil*, 2 vols., Arles: Actes Sud, 2000.

Guillon, Jean-Marie and Pierre Laborie, eds., *Mémoire et Histoire: la Résistance*, Toulouse: Privat, 1995.

Guillon, Jean-Marie and Robert Mencherini, eds., *La Résistance et les Européens du Sud*, Paris: L'Harmattan, 1999.

Guingouin, Georges, *Quatre ans de lutte sur le sol limousin*, Paris: Hachette, 1974.

Hawes, S. F. and White, R. T., eds., *Resistance in Europe, 1939–1945*, London: Allen Lane. 1975.

Hazareesingh, Sudhir, *Black Spartacus: The Epic Life of Toussaint Louverture*, London: Allen Lane, 2020.

Helm, Sarah, *A Life in Secrets: The Story of Vera Atkins and the Lost Agents of SOE*, London: Little, Brown, 2005.

Helm, Sarah, *If This is a Woman: Inside Ravensbrück, Hitler's Concentration Camp for Women*, London: Little, Brown, 2015.

Hessel, Stéphane, *Indignez-vous!*, Montpellier: Indigène éditions, 2010.

Hessel, Stéphane, *Engagez-vous: Entretiens avec Gilles Vanderpooten*, La Tour d'Aigues: Éditions de l'Aube, 2011.

Humbert, Agnès, *Notre Guerre: Souvenirs de Résistance*, Paris: Éditions Émile-Paul Frères, 1946. New edition Tallandier, 2004, Introduction by Julien Blanc. Translated with research and notes by Barbara Mellor and published as Humbert, Agnès, *Résistance: Memoirs of Occupied France*, London: Bloomsbury, 2008, with Afterword by Julien Blanc.

Jackson, Julian, *France: The Dark Years 1940–1944*, Oxford: Oxford University Press, 2001.

Jackson, Julian, *The Fall of France: The Nazi Invasion of 1940*, Oxford: Oxford University Press, 2003.

Jackson, Julian, *A Certain Idea of France: The Life of Charles de Gaulle*, London: Penguin/Allen Lane, 2018.

Jenkins, Ray, *A Pacifist at War: The Life of Francis Cammaerts*, London: Hutchinson, 2009.

Joutard, Philippe and François Marcot, *Les Étrangers dans la Résistance en France*, Besançon: Musée de la Résistance et de la Déportation, 1992.

Joutard, Philippe, Jacques Poujol, and Patrick Cabanel, eds., *Cévennes, Terre de Refuge, 1940–1944*, Montpellier: Presses du Languedoc, 1987.

Kaspi, André, Annie Kriegel, and Annette Wieviorka, eds., *Les Juifs de France dans la Seconde Guerre Mondiale*, Paris: Pardès No.16, Cerf, 1992.

Kedward, H. R., *Resistance in Vichy France: A Study of Ideas and Motivation in the Southern Zone 1940–1942*, Oxford: Oxford University Press, 1978.

Kedward, H. R., *In Search of the Maquis: Rural Resistance in Southern France, 1942–1944*, Oxford: Oxford University Press, 1993.

Kedward, Rod, *La Vie en Bleu: France and the French since 1900*, London: Allen Lane, Penguin, 2005.

Kedward, Roderick and Roger Austin, eds., *Vichy France and the Resistance: Culture and Ideology*, London: Croom Helm, 1985.

Kedward, H. R. and Nancy Wood, eds., *The Liberation of France: Image and Event*, Oxford and New York: Berg, 1995.

Kelly, Deborah and Martyn Cornick, eds., *A History of the French in London: Liberty, Equality, Opportunity*, London: Institute of Historical Research, 2013.

King, Stella, *"Jacqueline" [Yvonne Rudellat]: Pioneer Heroine of the Resistance*, London: Arms and Armour Press, 1989.

Kitson, Simon, *Vichy et la chasse aux espions Nazis 1940–1942: complexités de la politique de collaboration*, Paris: Autrement, 2005. Translated by Catherine Tihany as Kitson, Simon, *The Hunt for Nazi Spies: Fighting Espionage in Vichy France*, Chicago and London: University of Chicago Press, 2008.

Kitson, Simon, *Police and Politics in Marseille, 1936–1945*, Leiden/Boston: Brill, 2014.

Klarsfeld, Serge, *Vichy-Auschwitz: le rôle de Vichy dans la solution finale de la question juive en France*, Paris: Fayard, 2 vols., 1983–1985.

Kramer, Rita, *Flames in the Field: The Story of Four SOE Agents in Occupied France*, London: Michael Joseph, 1995.

Laborie, Pierre, *Résistants, Vichyssois et autres: l'évolution de l'opinion et des comportements dans le Lot de 1939 à 1945*, Paris: Éditions du CNRS, 1980.

Laborie, Pierre, *L'Opinion française sous Vichy*, Paris: Seuil, 1990.

Laborie, Pierre, *Penser l'événement, 1940–1945*, Édition de Cécile Vast et Jean-Marie Guillon, Paris: Gallimard, 2019.

Lacouture, Jean, *Le Témoignage est un combat: Une biographie de Germaine Tillion*, Paris: Seuil, 2000.

Latour, Anny, *La Résistance juive en France, 1940–44*, Paris: Stock, 1970.

Laub, Thomas J., *After the Fall: German Policy in Occupied France, 1940–1944*, Oxford: Oxford University Press, 2010.

Lazare, Lucien, *Rescue as Resistance: How Jewish Organizations Fought the Holocaust in France*, New York: Columbia University Press, 1996.

Lee, Daniel, *Pétain's Jewish Children: French Jewish Youth & the Vichy Regime, 1940–1942*, Oxford: Oxford University Press, 2014.

Lett, Brian, *S. O. E's Mastermind: An Authorized Biography of Major General Sir Colin Gubbins, KCMG, DSO, MC*, Barnsley: Pen and Sword Military, 2016.

Levisse-Touzé, Christine and Dominique Veillon, eds., *Résister sous l'Occupation: Libération-Nord 1940–1944*, Paris: La Documentation Française, 2013.

Mabon, Armelle, *Prisonniers de Guerre "Indigènes": Visages oubliés de la France occupée*, Paris: La Découverte, 2010.

Marcot, François, *La Résistance dans le Jura*, Besançon: Cêtre, 1985.

Marcot, François, ed., *La Résistance et les Français: Lutte armée et Maquis*, Paris: Les Belles Lettres, Annales littéraires de l'Université de Franche-Comté, vol. 617, 1996.

Marcot, François, ed., *Dictionnaire Historique de la Résistance*, Paris: Robert Laffont, 2006. (See note at the head of this Bibliography).

Marrus, Michael R. and Robert O. Paxton, *Vichy France and the Jews*, New York: Basic Books, 1981.

Martin, Helen, *Lot: Travels through a Limestone Landscape in Southwest France*, Wiltshire: Moho Books, 2008.

McCue, Paul, *Brighton's Secret Agents: The Brighton and Hove Contribution to Britain's WW2 Special Operations Executive (SOE)*, London: Uniform, 2016.

Mendès-France, Pierre, *The Pursuit of Freedom*, London: Longmans, Green and Co, 1956.

Michel, Henri, *Les courants de pensée de la Résistance*, Paris: Presses Universitaires de France, 1963.

Michel, Henri, *Bibliographie critique de la Résistance*, Paris: Institut Pédagogique National, 1964.

Michel, Henri, *Jean Moulin, l'unificateur*, Paris: Hachette, 1971.

Millar, George, *Maquis: An Englishman in the French Resistance*, London: Heinemann, 1945.

Missika, Dominique, *Berty Albrecht: Féministe et résistante*, Paris: Tempus, 2005.

Moore, Bob, ed., *Resistance in Western Europe*, Oxford and New York: Berg, 2000.

Moorehead, Caroline, *A Train in Winter: A Story of Resistance, Friendship and Survival*, London: Chatto & Windus, 2011.

Moorehead, Caroline, *Village of Secrets: Defying the Nazis in Vichy France*, London: Chatto & Windus, 2014.

Mulley, Clare, *The Spy who Loved: The Secrets and Lives of Christine Granville, Britain's First Female Special Agent of the Second World War*, London: Macmillan, 2012.

Nahas, Gabriel, *La Filière du Rail*, Paris: François-Xavier de Guibert, 1995.

Noiriel, Gérard, *Les origines républicaines de Vichy*, Paris: Hachette, 1999.

Nora, Pierre, ed., *Les Lieux de Mémoire*, 7 vols., Paris: Gallimard, 1984–1992, translated as *Realms of Memory: The Construction of the French Past*, 3 vols., New York: Columbia University Press, 1997.

Ott, Sandra, *War, Judgement, and Memory in the Basque Borderlands, 1914–1945*, Reno and Las Vegas: University of Nevada Press, 2008.

Ott, Sandra, ed., *War, Exile, Justice, and Everyday Life, 1936–1946*, Reno: Center for Basque Studies, University of Nevada, 2011.

Pattinson, Juliette, *Behind Enemy Lines: Gender, Passing and the Special Operations Executive in the Second World War*, Manchester: Manchester University Press, 2007.

Paxton, Robert O., *Vichy France: Old Guard and New Order, 1940–1944*, London: Barrie & Jenkins, 1972.

Pearson, Chris, *Scarred Landscapes: War and Nature in Vichy France*, London and New York: Palgrave Macmillan, 2008.

Pérotin, Yves dit Pothier, *La vie inimitable: Dans les maquis du Trièves et du Vercors en 1943 et 1944*, Grenoble: Presses universitaires de Grenoble, 2014.

Perrin, Nigel, *Spirit of Resistance: The Life of SOE Agent Harry Peulevé, DSO MC*, Barnsley: Pen & Sword, 2008.

Peschanski, Denis, *Des étrangers dans la Résistance*, Paris: Éditions de l'Atelier, 2002.

Peschanski, Denis and Jean-Louis Robert, eds., *Les Ouvriers en France pendant la Seconde Guerre mondiale*, Paris: IHTP, 1992.

Petitdemange, Francis and Jean-François Genet, *Les Passeurs: Des Lorrains anonymes dans la Résistance*, Nancy: Éditions de l'Est, 2003.

Pike, Robert, *Defying Vichy: Blood, Fear and French Resistance*, Stroud, Cheltenham: The History Press, 2018.

Pike, Robert, *Silent Village: Life and Death in Occupied France*, Cheltenham: The History Press, 2021.

Piketty, Guillaume, *Pierre Brossolette: un héros de la Résistance*, Paris: Odile Jacob, 1998.

Piketty, Guillaume, *Français en Résistance: Carnets de guerre, correspondance, journaux personnels*, Paris: Robert Laffont, 2009.

Poirier, Jacques, *The Giraffe Has a Long Neck*, Barnsley: Pen & Sword, 1995.

Pollard, Miranda, *Reign of Virtue: Mobilizing Gender in Vichy France*, Chicago: University of Chicago Press, 1998.

Posnanski, Renée, *Être juif en France pendant la Seconde Guerre mondiale*, Paris: Hachette, 1994.

Poujol, Jacques, *Protestants dans la France en Guerre, 1939–1945: Dictionnaire thématique et biographique*, Paris: Les Éditions de Paris, 2000.

Pour une histoire de l'Exil, français et belge, Paris: Bibliothèque de Documentation Internationale Contemporaine, *Matériaux pour l'histoire de notre temps*, No. 67, 2002.

Prost, Antoine, ed., *La Résistance, une histoire sociale*, Paris: Éditions de l'Atelier/Éditions ouvrières, 1997.

Purnell, Sonia, *A Woman of No Importance: The Untold Story of the American Spy Who Helped Win World War II, [Virginia Hall]*, New York: Viking, 2019.

Ravanel, Serge, *L'Esprit de Résistance*, Paris: Seuil, 1995.

Rayski, Adam, *Le choix des Juifs sous Vichy: Entre soumission et résistance*, Paris: La Découverte, 1992. Translated by Will Sayers as *The Choice of the*

Jews Under Vichy: Between Submission and Resistance, Notre Dame, Indiana, University of Notre Dame Press, 2005.

Rée, Jonathan, ed., *A Schoolmaster's War: Harry Rée, British Agent in the French Resistance*, New Haven and London: Yale University Press, 2020.

Rémy, Colonel, (Gilbert Renault), *Mémoires d'un Agent secret de la France Libre*, 3 vols., Paris: France-Empire, 1959–1961.

La Résistance et les Européens du Nord, Colloque international, Brussels: Centre de Recherches et d'Études historiques de la Seconde Guerre Mondiale, 1994.

La Résistance et les Européens du Sud: Pré-Actes, Aix-en-Provence: UMR Telemme, 1997.

Richards, Brooks, *Secret Flotillas*, 2 vols, London: Frank Cass, 2004.

Rioux, Jean-Pierre, Antoine Prost, and Jean-Pierre Azéma, *Les communistes français de Munich à Châteaubriant*, Paris: FNSP, 1987.

Robertson, K. G., ed., *War, Resistance & Intelligence: Essays in Honour of M. R. D. Foot*, Barnsley: Leo Cooper, 1999.

Rohrlich, Ruby, ed., *Resisting the Holocaust*, Oxford and New York: Berg, 1998.

Rossiter, Margaret L., *Women in the Resistance*, New York: Praeger, 1986.

Rougeyron, André, *Agents d'évasion: Imprimerie Alençonnaise*, 1947, trans. Marie-Antoinette McConnell as *Agents for Escape: Inside the French Resistance 1939–1945*, Baton Rouge: Louisiana State University Press, 1996.

Rouquet, François, *L'épuration dans l'administration française*, Paris: CNRS, 1993.

Roure, André, *Valeur de la Vie Humaine*, Paris: Sfelt, 1947.

Rousso, Henry, *Le Syndrome de Vichy 1944–198 . . .*, Paris: Seuil, 1987.

Ryan, Donna F., *The Holocaust & the Jews of Marseille*, Urbana and Chicago: University of Illinois Press, 1996.

Sainclivier, Jacqueline, *La Résistance en Ille et Vilaine, 1940–1944*, Rennes: Presses universitaires de Rennes, 1993.

Sainclivier, Jacqueline and Christian Bougeard, eds., *La Résistance et les Français: Enjeux stratégiques et environnement social*, Rennes: Presses universitaires de Rennes, 1995.

Schwartz, Paula, '"Redefining Resistance: The Activism of Women in Wartime France," in *Behind the Lines: Gender and the Two World Wars*, ed. Margaret Randolph Higonnet et al., New Haven: Yale University Press, 1987.

Schwartz, Paula, *Today Sardines Are Not for Sale: A Street Protest in Occupied Paris*, Oxford and New York: Oxford University Press, 2020.

Scott, James C., *Weapons of the Weak: Everyday Forms of Peasant Resistance*, Newhaven and London: Yale University Press, 1985.

Seaman, Mark, *Bravest of the Brave: The True Story of Wing Commander "Tommy" Yeo-Thomas, SOE Secret Agent, Codename "The White Rabbit,"* London: Michael O'Mara, 1997.

Seaman, Mark, *Special Operations Executive: A New Instrument of War*, London: Routledge, 2005.

Seaman, Mark, *Saboteur: The Untold Story of SOE's Youngest Agent at the Heart of French Resistance*, London: John Blake, 2018.

Semelin, Jacques, *Sans armes face à Hitler: La résistance civile en Europe, 1939–1945*, Paris: Payot, 1989. Translated by Suzan Husserl-Kapit as *Unarmed Against Hitler: Civilian Resistance in Europe, 1939–1943*, Westport, Connecticut and London: 1993.

Shennan, Andrew, *Rethinking France: Plans for Renewal 1940–1946*, Oxford: Clarendon Press, 1989.

Sivirine, Gleb (Lieutenant Vallier), *Le Cahier rouge du maquis: Journal de Résistance*, and Sivirine, Claude and Jean-Michel, *L'homme boussole: Témoignages*, with Guillon Jean-Marie, *Histoire du maquis Vallier*, Éditions Parole, 2007.

Soo, Scott, *The Routes to Exile, France and the Spanish Civil War refugees, 1939–2009*, Manchester: Manchester University Press, 2013.

Stafford, David, *Britain and European Resistance 1940–1945. A Survey of the Special Operations Executive, with Documents*, London: Macmillan, 1980.

Stein, Louis, *Beyond Death and Exile: The Spanish Republicans in France, 1939–1955*, Cambridge, Massachusetts and London: Harvard University Press, 1979.

Suberville, Gérald, *L'Autre Résistance*, Saint-Étienne-Vallée-Française: Aiou, 1998.

Sweets, John, *The Politics of Resistance in France, 1940–1944*, Chicago: Northern Illinois University Press, 1976.

Sweets, John, *Choices in Vichy France: The French Under Nazi Occupation*, Oxford and New York: Oxford University Press, 1986.

Tartakowsky, Danielle, *Les Manifestations de rue en France, 1918–1968*, Paris: Publications de la Sorbonne, 1997.

Taubmann, *L'Affaire Guingouin*, Limoges: Lucien Souny, 1994.

Taylor, Lynne, *Between Resistance and Collaboration: Popular Protest in Northern France*, London: Macmillan and New York: St. Martin's Press, 2000.

Tessier du Cros, Janet, *Divided Loyalties: A Scotswoman in Occupied France*, London: Hamish Hamilton, 1962. Paperback edition, Edinburgh: Canongate Classics, 1992.

Thoraval, Anne, *Paris, les lieux de la Résistance: La vie quotidienne de l'armée des ombres dans la capitale*, Paris: Parigramme, 2007.

Tickell, Jerrard, *Odette: The Story of a British Agent*, London: Chapman & Hall, 1949.

Tillon, Charles, *Les FTP*, Paris: Julliard, 1962.

Tollet, André, *La Classe ouvrière dans la Résistance*, Paris: Éditions sociales, 1984.

Vast, Cécile, *L'identité de la Résistance: Être résistant de l'Occupation à l'après-guerre*, Paris: Payot, 2010.

Vegh, Claudine, *Je ne lui ai pas dit au revoir. Des enfants de déportés parlent*, Paris: Gallimard, 1979.

Veillon, Dominique, *Le Franc-Tireur: Un journal clandestin, un mouvement de résistance 1940–1944*, Paris: Flammarion, 1977.

Veillon, Dominique, *Vivre et Survivre en France, 1937–1947*, Paris: Payot, 1995.

Verneret, Hubert, trans. Sarah Saunders and Patrick Depardon, *Teenage Resistance Fighter: With the Maquisards in Occupied France*, Oxford and Philadelphia: Casemate, 2017.

Viannay, Philippe, *Du bon usage de la France*, Paris: Ramsay, 1988.

Vinen, Richard, *The Unfree French: Life under the Occupation*. London: Penguin/Allen Lane, 2006.

Virgili, *La France "virile": Des femmes tondues à la liberation*, Paris: Payot, 2000.

Vistel, Alban, *Héritage spirituel de la Résistance*, Lyon: Lug, 1955.

Voldman, Danièle, ed., *La bouche de la vérité? La recherche historique et les sources orales*, Paris: Les Cahiers de l'IHTP. No.21, Nov.1992.

Vonau, Jean-Laurent, *Le procès de Bordeaux: Les Malgré-Nous et le drame d'Oradour*, Strasbourg: Éditions du Rhin, 2003.

Wake, Nancy, *The White Mouse*, London: Macmillan, 1985.

Walters, Anne-Marie, *Moondrop to Gascony*, London: Macmillan, 1946. New edition with Introduction, Postscript, and Notes by David Hewson: Wiltshire: Moho Books, 2009.

Weitz, Margaret Collins, *Sisters in the Resistance: How Women Fought to Free France, 1940–1945*, New York: John Wiley & Sons, 1995.

Wieviorka, Annette, *Ils étaient juifs, résistants, communistes*, Paris: Denoël, 1986.

Wieviorka, Olivier, *Une certaine idée de la Résistance: Défense de la France 1940–1949*, Paris: Seuil, 1995.

Wieviorka, Olivier, *Histoire de la Résistance, 1940–1945*, Paris: Perrin, 2013.

Wolikow, Serge, ed., *Les Images Collectives de la Résistance*, Dijon: Editions Universitaires de Dijon, 1997.

Wood, Nancy, *Germaine Tillion, une femme-mémoire: D'une Algérie à l'autre*, Traduit de l'anglais par Marie-Pierre Corrin, Paris: Autrement, 2003.

Zaretsky, Robert, *Nîmes at War: Religion, Politics and Public Opinion in the Gard, 1938–1944*, University Park, Pennsylvania State: University Press, 1995.

2. LITERATURE, ART, PHOTOGRAPHY, CINEMA

The range of insights into the resistance in France found in fiction, poetry, and film cannot easily be summarized, but such material is essential to the ways in which we talk about resistance. Such was the resistance role of imagination and inventiveness under the Occupation, and the subsequent importance of film in dramatizing people, places, and events, that Stéphane Hessel's emphasis on creativity, quoted at the end of the last chapter, must find a particular echo here. Not that historical and biographical writings lack imagination, far from it, but their sensitivity to accusations of being overinventive or incorrect make them cautious about evaluating the impact of fiction.

The clandestine publishing venture, Éditions de Minuit, based in Paris, was a resistance organization from 1942 until after the Liberation, whose stated aim was to produce and circulate high-quality literature, finely printed. Its first book of fiction, *Le Silence de la mer* by Vercors, was dedicated to the symbolist poet Saint-Pol-Roux, who died in the first days of the Occupation as a result of a drunken German soldier breaking into his Breton home, raping his daughter, and shooting the old governess. Fellow writers including the communist poet, Charles Aragon, labelled his death as an "assassination." The print run was small, but it was widely copied by hand, and its circulation by the time of the Liberation made it the classic it still is today.

It was reedited in London in 1943, again as the first book in a new series, *Les Cahiers du Silence*. In a shorter English translation by Cyril Connolly it was given the title, *Put Out the Light*, the words from Shakespeare's *Othello* that Vercors had put at the start of the second part of the novel in which the cultured German officer, Werner von Ebrennac, discovers the barbarism of his Nazi leaders. The identity of Vercors remained unknown until the Liberation, "the only real secret of the war," quipped Aragon. His name was finally revealed as Jean Bruller, writer, printer, and illustrator, who was the founder, with the writer Pierre de Lescure, of the Éditions de Minuit.

The enigma of the pseudonym, the complex imagery of silence, the drama of a male German occupier and a young woman of the house, and their shared values of European culture shattered by the barbarity of Nazism, have made this clandestine novel a constant talking point in understanding resistance. It is less about the nature of resistance and more about its necessity. Both its production and its story carried a moral imperative.

Many of the titles listed here can be seen to have either perpetuated or interrogated that imperative.

Added, Serge, *Le théâtre dans les années Vichy*, Paris: Ramsay, 1992.

Aragon, Louis, *Le Crève-Coeur*, London: Horizon-La France Libre, 1942.

Aragon, Louis, *Servitude et Grandeur des Français: Scènes des années terribles*, Paris: La Bibliothèque Française, 1945.

Atack, Margaret, *Literature and the French Resistance: Cultural politics and narrative forms 1940–1950*, Manchester: Manchester University Press, 1989.

Auxois [Édith Thomas], *Contes d'Auxois (Transcrit du Réel)*, Paris: Éditions de Minuit, 1943.

Bertin-Maght, Jean-Pierre, *Le cinéma sous l'Occupation*, Paris: Olivier Orban, 1989.

Bory, Jean-Louis, *Mon village à l'heure allemande*, Paris: Flammarion, 1945.

Camus, Albert, *Lettres à un ami allemand*, Paris: Gallimard, 1943/1948.

Camus, Albert, *La Peste*, Paris: Gallimard, 1947, translated by Stuart Gilbert as *The Plague*, London: Hamish Hamilton, 1948.

Cévennes [Jean Guéhenno], *Dans la Prison*, Paris: Éditions de Minuit, 1944.

Chabrol, Jean-Pierre, *Un Homme de Trop*, Paris: Gallimard, 1958.

Chadwyck-Healey, Charles, *Literature of the Liberation: The French Experience in Print 1944–1946*, Cambridge: Cambridge University Library, 2014.

Cone, Michèle C., *Artists under Vichy: A Case of Prejudice and Persecution*, Princeton: Princeton University Press, 1992.

Curtis, Jean-Louis, *Les Forêts de la Nuit*, Paris: Julliard, 1947.

Daniel, Laurent [Elsa Triolet], *Les Amants d'Avignon*, Paris: Éditions de Minuit, 1943.

Debû-Bridel, Jacques, *Les Éditions de Minuit: Historique*, Paris: Éditions de Minuit, 1945.

Delbo, Charlotte, *La mémoire et les jours*, Paris: Berg International, 1995.

Eluard, Paul, *Poésie et Vérité 1942*, New Edition, Neuchâtel: La Baconnière, 1943.

Faulks, Sebastien, *Charlotte Gray*, London: Hutchinson, 1988.

Forez [François Mauriac], *Le Cahier Noir*, Paris: Éditions de Minuit, 1943.

French Writing on English Soil: A Choice of French Writing Published in London Between November 1940 and June 1944. Selected and translated by J. C. Weightman, London: Sylvan Press, 1945.

Frenkel, Françoise, *No Place to Lay One's Head*, Preface by Patrick Modiano, Translated from the French by Stephanie Smee, London: Pushkin Press, 2018.

Frey, Hugo, *Louis Malle*, Manchester and New York: Manchester University Press, 2004.

Frey, Hugo, *Nationalism and the Cinema in France: Political Mythologies and Film Events, 1945–1995*, New York and Oxford: Berghahn Books, 2014.

Gille, Elisabeth, *Le mirador: Mémoires rêvés: Irène Némirovsky 1903–1942*, Paris: Presses de la Renaissance, 1992.

Hayward, Susan and Vincendeau, Ginette, eds., *French Film: Texts and Contexts*, 2nd ed., London and New York: Routledge, 2000.

Higgins, Ian, ed., *Anthology of Second World War Poetry*, London: Methuen, 1982. Later edition, University of Glasgow French & German Publications, 1994.

L'Honneur des Poètes, Paris: Éditions de Minuit, 1943.

Jean, Raymond, *Paul Eluard par lui-même*, Paris: Seuil, 1968.

Joffo, Joseph, *Un Sac de Billes*, Paris: J. -C. Lattès, 1973. Edition with introduction and notes by P. A. Brooke, London: Routledge, 1989.

Kessel, Joseph, *L'armée des ombres*, Paris: Plon, 1963.

Kimyongür, Angela, *Memory and Politics: Representations of War in the Work of Louis Aragon*, Cardiff: University of Wales Press, 2007.

Langlois, Suzanne, *La Résistance dans le cinéma français 1944–1994, de La Libération de Paris à Libera me*, Paris-Montreal: L'Harmattan, 2001.

Lindeperg, Sylvie, *Les Écrans de l'ombre: La Seconde Guerre mondiale dans le cinéma français (1944–1969)*, Paris: Éditions du CNRS, 1997.

Malle, Louis and Modiano, Patrick, *Lacombe Lucien: Un film de Louis Malle, Script*, Paris: Gallimard, 1974.

Mawer, Simon, *The Girl Who Fell from the Sky*, London. Little, Brown, 2012.

Minervois [Claude Aveline], *Le Temps Mort*, Paris: Éditions de Minuit, 1944.

Morpurgo, Michael, *In the Mouth of the Wolf, Brother, Father, Teacher, Spy, [Francis Cammaerts]*. Illustrated by Barroux, London: Egmont, 2018.

Mosse, Kate, *Citadel*, London: Orion Books, 2012.

Némirovsky, Irène, *Suite Française*, Paris: Denoël, 2004.

Noir, Jean [Jean Cassou], *33 Sonnets composés au secret, présentés par François La Colère*, Paris: Éditions de Minuit, 1944.

Ophuls, Marcel, *The Sorrow and the Pity: Chronicle of a French City under German Occupation*, Film script translated by Mireille Johnston, Introduction by Stanley Hoffman, St.Albans: Paladin, 1975.

Parrot, Louis and Jean Marcenac, *Paul Eluard*, Paris: Seghers, 1964.

Paulhan, Jean, *Lettre aux Directeurs de la Résistance*, Paris: Éditions de Minuit, 1952.

Pessis, Jacques, *La Bataille de Radio Londres, 1940–1944, Jacques Pessis nous présente "Les Français parlent aux Français," 70e anniversaire de l'Appel du 18 juin*, Paris: Omnibus, 2010.

Philipponnat, Olivier and Patrick Lienhardt, *La Vie d'Irène Némirovsky*, Paris: Grasset, Denoël, 2007.

Sapiro, Gisèle, *La Guerre des écrivains, 1940–1953*, Paris: Fayard, 1999.

Sartre, Jean-Paul, *Théatre: Les Mouches, Huis-Clos, Morts sans Sépulture, La Putain respectueuse*, Paris: Gallimard, 1947.

Sartre, Jean-Paul, *Iron in the Soul (La Mort dans l'âme)*, London: Hamish Hamilton, 1950.

Seghers, Pierre, *La Résistance et ses poètes*, Éditions Seghers, 1974.

Sheers, Owen, *Resistance*, London: Faber and Faber, 2007.

Simonin, Anne, *Les Éditions de Minuit: Le devoir d'insoumission (1942–1955)*, Paris: IMEC, 1994.

Thomson, Rupert, *Never Anyone but You*, London: Corsair, 2018.

Vaillant, Roger, *Drôle de jeu*, Paris: Buchet-Chastel, 1977.

Valland, Rose, *Le Front de l'Art, Défense des collections françaises*, Paris: Réunion des musées nationaux-Grand Palais, 2014.

Vercors [Jean Bruller], *Le Silence de la mer*, Paris: Éditions de Minuit, 1942.
Vercors [Jean Bruller], *La Bataille du Silence*, Paris: Presses de la Cité, 1967.
  English edition, *The Battle of Silence: An Autobiography by the Author of "The
  Silence of the Sea,"* London and Glasgow: Collins, 1968.
Weiss, Jonathan, *Irène Némirovsky, Biographie*, Paris: Éditions du Félin, 2005.
Zaretsky, Robert, *Albert Camus: Elements of a Life*, Ithaca and London: Cornell
  University Press, 2010.

3. FILM TITLES AND DIRECTORS

Allied, Robert Zemeckis, 2016.
L'Armée des ombres (Army of the Shadows), Jean-Pierre Melville, 1969.
Les armes de l'esprit (Weapons of the Spirit), Pierre Sauvage, 1989.
The Army of Crime, Robert Guédiguian, 2008.
Au revoir les enfants, Louis Malle, 1987.
La Bataille du Rail, René Clément, 1946.
Blanche et Marie, Jacques Renard, 1985.
Boulevard des hirondelles, Josée Yanne, 1991–3.
Carve Her Name With Pride, Lewis Gilbert. 1958.
Casablanca, Michael Curtiz, 1942.
Le Chagrin et la Pitié (The Sorrow and the Pity), Marcel Ophuls, 1969/1971.
Charlotte Gray, Gillian Armstrong, 2002.
Colette, Anthony Giacchino, Guardian Documentaries, 2020.
Un condamné à mort s'est échappé (A Man Escaped), Robert Bresson, 1956.
Le Dernier Métro (The Last Metro), François Truffaut, 1980.
Escape to Victory, John Huston, 1981.
Les Femmes de l'Ombre, Jean-Paul Salomé, 2008.
Le Grand Charles, Bernard Stora, 2005.
La Grande Vadrouille, Gérard Oury, 1966.
To Have and Have Not, Howard Hawks, 1945.
Un Héros Très Discret (A Self-Made Hero), Jacques Audiard, 1996.
Hiroshima Mon Amour, Alain Resnais, 1959.
Un Homme de Trop (Shock Troops), Costa-Gavras, 1967.
Jéricho, Henri Calef, 1946.
Jeux interdits, René Clément, 1952.
Johnny Frenchman, Charles Frend, 1945.
Lacombe Lucien, Louis Malle, 1974.
Laissez-Passer (Safe Conduct), Bertrand Tavernier, 2001.
Libres Français de Londres, Timothy Miller, 2010.
La ligne de démarcation, Claude Chabrol, 1966.
Lucie Aubrac, Claude Berri, 1997.
Memoir of War, Emmanuel Finkiel, 2019.
Monsieur Klein, Joseph Losey, 1976.
The Monuments Men, George Clooney, 2014.
No Ordinary People, Mike Fox, Foxy Films, 1995.
Now It Can Be Told, R. A. F. Film Production Unit, 1946.
Nuit et Brouillard (Night and Fog), Alain Resnais, 1955.

Odette, Herbert Wilcox, 1950.
Oubliés et Trahis, Les prisonniers de guerre coloniaux, Violaine Dejoie-Robin and
    Armelle Mabon, 2003.
Papy fait de la Résistance, Jean-Marie Poiré, 1983.
Paris brûle-t-il? René Clément, 1966.
Le Père tranquille (Mr Orchid), René Clément, 1946.
The Plague, Luis Puenzo, 1992.
Un Sac de Billes, Christian Duguay, 2017.
Schindler's List, Steven Spielberg, 1993.
Section Spéciale, Costa-Gavras. 1975.
Shoah, Claude Lanzmann, 1985.
Le Silence de la Mer, Jean-Pierre Melville, 1949.
Suite Française, Saul Dibb, 2015.
Des "terroristes" à la retraite, Mosco, 1985.
The Train, John Frankenheimer, Burt Lancaster, Arthur Penn, 1965.
La Traversée de Paris, Claude Autant-Lara, 1956.
Uranus, Claude Berri, 1990.

4. WEBSITES

Musée de la Résistance Nationale (MRN): http://www.museedelaresistance
    enligne.org
Musée de la Libération de Paris - musée du general Leclerc - musée Jean
    Moulin: https://www.museeliberation-leclerc-moulin.paris.fr
Mémorial de la Shoah. 17, rue Geoffroy l'Asnier, 75004 Paris: http://www
    .memorialdelashoah.org
Mémoire Vive de la Résistance: www.mvr.asso.fr
Archive of Resistance Testimony, University of Sussex: https://www.thekeep.info
    /collections/keep-partners/university-of-sussex-special-collections/archive-of
    -resistance-testimony/
Hanna Diamond's website on the Exode of 1940: http://www.fleeinghitler.org
David Harrison's website on SOE F section: www.soe-french.co.uk
Alan Latter's website on Resistance in SW France: http://resistancefrancaise
    .blogspot.com/
Imperial War Museum: http://www.iwm.org.uk
Allied Forces Heritage Group/ Groupe du Patrimoine des Forces Alliées: info@
    afheritage.org
Secret WW2 Learning Network: https://www.secret-ww2.net

Index